DEAD TO ME

HOLLYWOOD

Mario Quinones-Revolori

BEN LORINES PUBLISHING
11012 Ventura Blvd Unit 135
Studio City, CA 91604

Hotline: 818-602-5554
Facebook: Ben Lovorines
Email: mariochosen123@gmail.com
              mario2qr@gmail.com

Ordering information:
Quantity Sales. Special discounts are available on quantity purchases by corporations, associations, and others. For details, contact the publisher at the address above.

Library of Congress Control Number: IN PROCESS
ISBN: 978-1-5136-6554-2

Dedication

For Ben Revolori, whose spirit of peace shines brightly every day.

For Allison Hernandez, whose physical and spiritual guidance gave me the strength to write this touching and inspirational true story.

Acknowledgments

I wish to acknowledge with deepest gratitude and no small degree of pride the help and contribution of the following:

Reina M Hernandez
Terry Nevin
Uriel Argueta
Luis E Flores
Julio A Orellana
Joaquin Jovcl

I would like to express my sincerest thanks to many people, especially Jorge Zuniga, whose caring and support provided the room to make the ideas possible; Rene Najarro, who continually showed me how to keep focused when there were a thousand things to do; Anna Revolori, for many stimulating ideas, and for suggesting the title and the front cover; Margarita Guzman for the exploration of many options, including the encouragement to write, a mentor showing the subtle side of creativity.

Finally, I owe a debt of gratitude to my sons Tony Revolori and Mario Revolori, whose unique contribution stimulates appreciation, and Ben Revolori, for appealing the layout of the book.

Contents

Chosen I Am

Captain Daniel Knus, AKA Danny Knus, a retired general, self-employed in the landscaping business, is a fat sixty-eight years of age with three of his upper teeth missing. He knocked at the door seven times, and he stopped. I opened the door and heard him saying to himself, "Dead To Me." He kept staring at the withering flowers and the dead bushes around my house. I met him for the first time that morning. He tried to persuade me to hire him on the spot for the gardening and landscaping position that I had placed on the Orange County Register. We talked for ten minutes about how much he was going to charge me to water and mow the lawn twice a week.

After we sealed the deal, Knus changed the subject, and he began with the story of a nine-year-old boy; he didn't ask me if I had time and wanted to hear it. Curiously, he picked by chance – or on purpose – my last name for his main character. He started spitting saliva from his missing teeth-gap every time he opened his mouth, chewing and talking at the same time. Knus said, "One day, the little boy came to talk to me." He started with a punchline, "This lonely boy was little B. M. Revolori, a sad story," he whispered in my ear. "I was twenty-three when I met him. I didn't have any idea why he came to speak with me about his troubles. Perhaps he thought he could trust me. The truth is, he felt protected around me. Surely, he eased up his pain by telling me his problem. His feet were blistered, bleeding, and dirty." Knus said to me that Revolori told him, "'I walk every morning and every afternoon along Saint Nicholas Brook. I'm afraid, deadly afraid all the time. I feel that behind my back, the shadow of death engulfs my body. I see scary faces floating in the air, and they frighten me too. Thunderous voices come to whistle to my ears without stopping; they scare me to death. I call out loudly for help, and I run as fast as I can to a nearby abandoned shack every single time, but no one hears me or comes to help me.

Every time I come back home, my dad is waiting for me. He greets me with a big loving and caring hug, but I don't dare to tell him anything. I keep the events a secret; I have never told anyone about it. I know I have been chosen by two forces: the light of goodness, and the shadows of darkness.

"Now, I'll make the best choices to solve any problem. Of course, it'll take me a great deal of thinking and a long time to make my mind up.

"I have been followed by good and evil all of my life. As far as I remember, I've always been on the run to escape the shadows of death. I'm living in a tough world. Five months ago, I tried to talk to my dad, but he just told me not to listen to those voices and nonsense imaginings. He said that they were wind noises just playing tricks on me. Since then, I didn't know where to go to ask for help. But a week after I asked my dad, I decided to take a chance and went to tell my mom. I went into the small kitchen where she was cooking. I took the opportunity, and I began to tell her part of the story. Immediately after, she stared at me. She interrupted and stopped me, raising her right hand and crossing herself. She asked me to give her a hand with the dishes. I guess she was being a good mother. She told me to pray and to ask the Lord to find a solution to my problems, and she crossed herself a second time."

Revolori, after a long pause, continued, "My life had been hell for the last thirty-nine months. I thought my mother gave me a good piece of advice. And my life took a turn and changed for the better. Now, new thoughts overwhelmed my mind. I know I have met the Lord and also the devil. Now I'm sure I am going to go through many tough times in my life. These are the feelings that will be in my heart, and all these warnings have been revealed to me through dreams, prophesies, revelations, and visions. I know I'm sounding like a fanatic religious kid, but I'm not. I dreamed what I dreamed, and I saw what I saw. I'm always truthful to myself and to others.

"Three months after I spoke with my mom, I met my partner for life. He told me to go deep into the forest every afternoon to talk to him. Till then, I had always chosen a special hiding place where I knew no one could see or hear me when I asked my new invisible friend how to deal with my problems. The Lord gives me visions and interpretations. Of course, I carefully choose every single step I take because I'm sure that the forces of darkness are watching me, and they want to control my destiny. Evil spirits are always chasing me around and waiting for the right time to entrap me. They want to turn me into a demon to worship Satan, and to walk in darkness for the rest of my life. Lucifer invites me to join his team of evildoers. But I am chosen to follow the light."

Revolori took a long pause to catch his breath, then he proceeded, "One day my mind told me that I was caught in between four tall walls that I couldn't climb up to get out because they were very high. I couldn't move forward either; it was too dark inside, and there was not enough room to take a step in any direction. A voice called out to me; it was so loud, and it frightened me. The sound came down from the very top. Slowly, I lifted my face, and I dared to look up. I saw no one. I fell on my knees, and I kissed the ground. I was sure that I had only one way out, or only one direction to go. I had to take control of my mind and use wisely the little strength I had left. I had to do it all by myself; there was no other way that I could think of or take. I thought the only chance to win was if I prayed and asked my invisible friend to help me, for he was there by my side and always ready to guide me and fight for me. I was certain that by trusting the Lord, I could defeat my enemy blindfolded in the darkness. It wasn't going to be easy, but I had the will and the power to give the devil a tough fight. And this way, my destiny has guided me around the first nine years of my life, till this very moment. To me, it had lasted for eternity, but in reality, the hard times had begun four years back. Three weeks ago, I celebrated my ninth birthday without a birthday party or a cake." Revolori stopped to clear his throat, and he ended his childhood story.

Fifteen years passed, the time flew by so fast, and Revolori became a young adult. Of course, Knus kept a close friendship with him from the very first day he met him. Revolori kept him posted by telling him new stories of his personal life every single month. One time, Revolori stood up while he was cleaning his eyes with a spotless and well-pressed handkerchief, and he said, "At the beginning of my adult life, I was into sports, arts, and music. I loved the entertainment industry. I hate math, science, and physics so much; these subjects I just don't care for. I flunked every time I took science- and math-related exams in high school. During my years at the university, I struggled to pass the midterms and finals. By the way, I graduated with a Bachelor of Arts in English and Spanish literature.

"In college, my nickname was Morris, and I thought my true identity was lost forever. But the impossible happened when I turned twenty-three. I was at a botany lab class when I realized how cool my real name is, and I started to use it again, because it is a powerful name that my parents had given me from birth to death. They named me B. M. Revolori. Everyone I had met thought that my mother was a religious fanatic when she picked my name, but I was proud of it because she gave me two great Bible names. At least for me, that was a gift. And I knew it was cool that my parents had chosen Benjamin Matthew. And it was just fine with me. I'm still dreaming of hitting the jackpot one day. It has given me an identity, a reason to be myself and to be on my own to make wise decisions. Now I'm prepared to deal with any problem as it comes, no matter how tough it gets. In the past, I couldn't face the unknown, and darkness was my worst phobia. I had panic attacks every time I found myself alone in the dark."

This is a true story that Danny Knus started to tell me that morning. It was the beginning of his endless tale. Knus was going to be my gardener for many years. He sat on the cement in the middle of the driveway for a minute. He told me, "I'll never stop, and I'll pick a new story every week. I'm going to recount Revolori's unique and touching inspirational true story once a week for many weeks, months, and years to come."

I had planned to run an errand after signing the contract. I didn't want to stay home, but I was glad that Knus stopped me when I was walking to my car, and he chose me to be his audience.

The Truth

The following week, Knus showed up early in the morning. I didn't expect that he was always going to be chewing some kind of greasy food mixed with tobacco leaves and dropping saliva down his lower lip. I asked him what he was munching on. But he just gave me a look. I understood I could not get an answer from him. Obviously, he wanted me to listen to his next story. I accepted the invitation, for I had plenty of time to spare that day. He focused and started to tell me a new story passed down to him by Revolori himself. "I was told by teachers and by my father to tell the truth no matter what. In my thoughts, these words echoed every time I had a conversation with anyone, and no lie slipped out of my mouth, so I thought." Knus paused for a second and took a deep breath. And I asked myself, *What's going on? How can people around the world be encouraged to tell the truth?* Knus looked at me and gave me a smile, and continued. Revolori said, "I see programs on television, I listen to the radio, I read newspapers, and follow all media platforms and I hear many lies that they tell to promote the product that is being offered." I stopped Knus for a second; I had no choice, and I dared to ask him to give me a break to go get a glass of water to take a pill for my migraine headache and allergies. When I came back, I made myself comfortable to listen to Revolori's story narrated to me by my new friend Knus. I sat and rested my back on the garage's wall and sharpened my ears to hear the rest of the tale. Knus told me that Revolori looked him straight in his eyes and he said, "When I speak with my friends and answer questions…" Revolori stopped and became silent. He took a breath, then he said, "Out of a hundred replies I say, several lies are counted against my clean record, but other people's lies are doubled or tripled compared with my fibs. Politicians try to be honest and fair. They promise not to lie and to tell the truth. As a matter of fact, it is a false promise to manipulate voters. Politicians' promises are fake to get votes and to manipulate their rigged campaigns. If we count their lies, probably, they rank to be much higher than ordinary people. Surely, politicians lie to get elected.

"In sports—I don't care what kind of sport, soccer, football, basketball, baseball, and others—some owners, coaches, and players are looking for the big piece of the pie. They don't tell the truth to their fans; they cheat to make an extra buck. I'm talking about many coaches, owners, and athletes; they are always crooks, cheaters, and liars. They have a business to run, and they have a big group of hungry fans to feed with lies, and a profitable product to sell. The world revolves around lies, and no one tells the truth. Mrs. Ruth Green, my elementary school teacher, encouraged me to speak the truth and to be honest. Back in the days when I didn't know that much about honesty, but I was certain she was not honest herself, I used to ask myself, 'Are all people liars?' I often had these questions in my mind. Later on, I came to the conclusion that we are all liars, big-time liars. People are just selling, and they need to keep their jobs to get their paychecks coming every week. My father told me many times, 'If I ever catch you lying, I will burn your mouth with the flame of a lighter.' Ironically, I caught my dad a few times lying to my brothers, to my mother, and to me. I knew he had been having an affair with a married woman, who happened to be Mrs. Ruth Green, my third-grade teacher. But he lied to cover up from the rumor spreading around.

"Well, the whole world is a mess; no one tells the truth. It only happens in courts in the minds of judges and lawyers. When they make people recite what they want to hear, and they ask, 'Do you promise to tell the whole truth and nothing but the truth so help you God?' And as soon as the witness opens his or her mouth, the magic line comes out: 'Yes, I do, Your Honor.' But judges, lawyers, and witnesses know they are not telling the truth; they're not speaking from the heart but by mechanical movement of their mouths. I don't expect to hear the truth all the time. In fact, no one would speak the truth ever. I know it is not possible. Let's talk about the great prophets of the Bible. If I have the chance to go back in time to interview them, right now or even in the past, certainly I will not get from them the whole truth. They were humans just like us. We are simply made of flesh and blood, and corruption will always be our nature. For example, King David lied about the Bathsheba affair, and worse, he tried to cover it up and justified the killing of her husband, Uriah. I think the best way to deal with this problem that we all face in the world is to admit the burden we carry on our shoulders and understand that we cannot be truthful, and more than one time a day, we lie. Nonetheless, we should try our best to make the change.

"We have the power to control our own lives. We can help a little, and we should work hard to make the best choices and to pick the best options. I strongly believe we should push our strengths to teach others and ourselves about honesty. I think admitting that we always lie and that we every so often hide the truth will help. We must think back and forth, knowing that we can do better if we try. Many times, we ignore the problem until it becomes bigger and harder to solve. The difficulties and the puzzles we face in our lives, we need to correct, to control, and to repair. We must give ourselves a pat on our backs and be smart to bring the truth to our minds. If we lie, we are not honest with ourselves. We have an incurable disease, and that sickness will contaminate and destroy us." At this point, Knus stopped for a second. I raised my eyes to heaven, and then I brought them back to look at him, and I whispered to myself, "Revolori had a lot of wisdom, or he was making up the story." Knus noticed and smiled; he took over the conversation again.

He said, "To be honest with you, it is a privilege to tell you BM's stories, and you must register them in the deepest of your brain and seal them in your heart." Knus continued telling me the story. Revolori nodded two times and said, "We human beings should encode from birth in our memory the word truth and learn to apply it early in life. We must have good attitudes, and if we are honest, it is possible to tell the truth most of the time. I'm working hard every minute to tell the truth. I accomplish it at least ninety-eight percent of the time. I search for spiritual guidance very often, but still, I fall short, and I cannot be truthful all the time because my tongue urges me to be a liar. I insist that this is a problem we'll take to our death beds, and we can't clean it up completely. But there are leaders we can study to learn more.

"For example, Jesus Christ always spoke about love and peace, but he also preached, 'I am the way, the truth, and the life; whoever comes to me will have salvation and eternal life.' Jesus himself is the only man who's known to speak nothing but the truth. Can anyone say, 'I am the way, the truth, and the life?' This question will remain unanswered for years to come, and it will be hidden for eternity. I'm a big supporter when it comes to speaking the truth, but I'm not totally truthful myself. I've got to admit, I'm getting wiser in doing many things right. I set my mind to think before I reply, but the true answer is not close to being truthful. Neither my heart nor my brain has found an easy way to disentangle the enigma of truthfulness. Big corporations sell applications to consumers who want to learn how to spend time on computers and other electronic devices. And these programs mess up their lives. Certainly, their learning is without knowledge to their own brains; at least they should stop to think and to have a better understanding of the products they are purchasing. There is no doubt in my mind they have faith in the new technology, but they are learning without wisdom, without honesty. They are wasting away their brains, and at the end of the day, they will regret when they learn that they are misled, and they are not getting wisdom or intelligence to stand up to become producers."

Revolori took another break. He watered his chapped lips and smiled. "I have traveled in many countries on four continents, and I haven't found a single person who has told me the truth a hundred percent. Poor people hope and dream of enjoying the lifestyle of the rich and famous. But the wealthy and government leaders manipulate poor people, and this is one of the reasons we are addicted to telling lies. None of us will stop lying in our lifetime, end of discussion. In every country I've been to, I have talked to natives who live in the countryside, and also to those who are from the cities. There is a special reason why I have chosen to interview people who reside in big cities and those who live in rural areas. One, the levels of education between the two groups vary. But no matter what their education is, when I ask them questions within the conversation, they give me almost the same response. The vocabulary they use to answer is different, but not the answers. No one tells the truth, and nobody could pass my test. We find people everywhere in the world who don't tell the truth. They keep secrets to themselves, but they talk about things that are helpful and good for them. Two, the time they took to give me their answers was ages apart. City people rushed to give me the answers because they did not have much time to spend with me. In the villages, they welcomed me to sit and have a cup of coffee or a cup of tea. And they even invited me to spend the night in their homes. Sometimes we chatted all night. But, when they answered, they gave me the same answers. They didn't tell me the truth when I asked them questions that they didn't want to hear, or when the answer would not be correct. On one occasion, I was on a long flight to India. I was traveling on Cathay Airlines. The plane was completely booked, and roughly eighty percent of the passengers were Asians, nineteen percent Indians, and one percent Europeans and Americans. I was having a long conversation with the passenger sitting next to me, who was an Indian fellow. During the flight, he talked about the history of India from ancient times to the present. He spoke about religion, and about their giant neighbor, and the enmity between his home country India and China. Finally, we landed in Mumbai. I have to say, I had a good time during the flight. I learned a great deal about China and India, thanks to the great conversation I had with the Indian passenger who sat to my right. As I always do, when I gather new information, immediately, I checked it out for authenticity. This time after doing my own research, all he shared with me was about sixty percent lies. I was certain he gave me the wrong information on purpose.

"Certainly, we have to be aware of the meaning of honesty. We must do our best to tell the truth, not to lie that much, and to respect the gift of truth that gives strength to the heart and teaches us to live in harmony and to respect one another. The spiritual and physical healing will connect the brain and the heart when we choose to tell the truth. And when we give truthful answers to most or all the questions that we have to reply to in our daily conversations, then the true healing will start to pour as rain falling to water the fields all over the world to plant the seeds of truth. But only the true achievers will have a very small chance to grasp the real meaning of being truthful." Knus rested and told me, "This is what young Revolori shared with me on the topic of truth."

Wheel Riders

It was cloudy that day. Knus took his break later than his normal time. I was exhausted, and I didn't have enough energy to listen to his stories. I was avoiding him the whole time. Suddenly, I heard his voice outside; steps were coming close to the front door. I opened the drapes and saw the old man chewing and salivating fast. He had a drop of grease rolling down the right corner of his lower lip. I pushed the door to open it and went out. I followed him and sat next to him. He stretched out his arms, and with a soft voice, he began, once again, telling me what Revolori had told him: "The dream continues for some young adults around the world to become rich and famous. These dreams of success start at eight years of age for some children." Knus took a huge bite of his double cheeseburger. He offered me a bite, and I politely refused the offer. He went on with the adventure. Revolori said, "I met a girl. She was nine years old, and she touched my heart in a very special way, maybe for the rest of my life. But I will tell you about her story in a future meeting."

Revolori continued, "In our lifetime, we learn to read, to repeat words, and to watch events that have been discovered by someone else, and very few people attempt to become creators, inventors, producers, and leaders. For example, President Obama climbed up to become the first black president of the most powerful nation in the history of the world, not only one term but for two administrations. And if he accomplished his goal, we could, we should, and we would too. We must work hard to become part of a legend, to guide and lead our children to follow their dreams for a better future. So new generations get better than the one before, and they'll be part of history-making, and they'll become peacemakers to save the world."

"Listen good!" Knus yelled, "this is the best part about what Revolori told me." And he went on to tell me that Revolori said, "A couple of young adults approached me on a short ride by train from San Diego to Los Angeles. They had a great story, and they chose me to pass it on. And I was honored to share these two brothers' real-life ordeal. The brothers wanted to remain anonymous; I will not use their real names, but I'll give them fake ones.

"The older brother, I'll call Marc Paulo, and his younger brother, I will name David Paulo. These two brothers recited me the horrible attack that occurred to them when they were eleven and twelve years of age. Marc started, 'We were walking downtown in a big city in a Latin American country. It was early in the morning.' Then Marc, a stalky boy, came closer and whispered, 'We don't want anybody else to hear.' He proceeded, 'We halted at a bus stop. We were standing and waiting for the next local bus to take us back home. All of a sudden, I took a step to the right, and I saw a man staring at me. He was about twelve inches away from my face. Then I turned to the left, for I was trying to find a way to escape. I ended up face-to-face with another scary man. And I went back a few inches, but a hand pushed me forward. I wanted to run, but a barrel of a gun was pointed at my face, making contact with my forehead. I chose to fight them, to defend myself, but David raised his hands up in defeat. A scar-faced man grabbed me and put me in cuffs in a blink of an eye. I didn't see where my brother was taken, but he had disappeared, and that was the truth. I looked everywhere, but my eyes couldn't spot him in the multitude walking in the busy, dirty street. I was dragged down the streets while bystanders waved me good-bye. They knew what was going to happen to me. The two guys who were dragging me laughed and stopped for a second. They waved back to the crowd, then they turned to me. One of them said, "We are going to tie your groin and then hang you high. No way back; it is a one-way ticket. You're dead!" A minute later, I was thrown face-down on the floor of a jeep with a government license plate. The driver was reading a newspaper, resting his elbows on the steering wheel. To my surprise, David was already on the vehicle's floor, and the cuffs were still fastened on his wrists. I was in shock to see my brother pinned to the metal. There was my little bro moaning in pain. I took a big breath, although I was so happy to see David still alive. I thought that was the last time we would ever see the daylight again. David looked me in the eye, and a few tears ran down his cheeks. The newspaperman turned to us and asked us a couple of questions. Honestly, we answered him, and we were released immediately for no apparent reason. Or maybe we told him what he wanted to hear. We'll never know it. But Jesus used the newspaper reader to save us from death.'"

Revolori, almost in tears, went on, "And based on all the information the brothers gave me, I can clearly imagine that they told me the truth. My heart just couldn't take it after I heard the tribulations that these innocent boys had faced when they were still teenagers. What bothered me the most was that it was a horrible attack by secret peace officers, who clearly misused and abused their power. My heart goes out to them, and to millions of young people who receive similar punishments from government employees and police officers in every country of the world."

Revolori sighed, took a breath, shook his head, and continued. "The truth of the matter is that those in power mistreat the working class. Ordinary people don't have a chance to defend themselves from the corruption of government personnel, powerful criminals, and from wealthy people. The criminals will never stop, no matter how hard these poor people work; day and night, the mistreatment to these helpless and hopeless men and women will not end. Their suffering will never end. They will never stop torturing the innocent to protect and cover up for those individuals in power. I know nothing will change in this world. The wealthy, criminals, and powerful people have established a crooked system to govern and rule with a rod and a sword from the beginning of mankind. Respectfully, I'm not against powerful people or government personnel, but against the mistreatment and abuse of power to hurt people who can't make enough money to put food on the table to feed their hungry children. Usually, they're weak because of their financial status, and their opportunities are limited.

"I strongly believe the ride through life is special and unique, and so different for everybody. Some people are raised with all the wealth in the world and enjoy it from birth to death. Others make their own fortune by working very hard and saving every penny they make. They are true achievers, and they know how to set their minds to work and save. Still others try so hard but do not have the mental ability to increase their wealth, and no matter how much they earn, they'll spend more than what they make. There is also a large group, and the majority of the people in the world fit in it. These people work all the time, but it seems they never earn enough money to buy a home and pay their bills. They just make enough to cover their expenses. Is it bad luck? No one knows. All I can say is that's my case too, and I work hard every single day. I'm getting old and close to finishing the race, but I still don't see my bank account piling up a big amount of cash. And I feel I'm almost ready to give up my fight.

"Life will always be unfair, but there is plenty for everybody. He who takes the chances and works wisely will become rich. For sure, he who doesn't work hard, and spoils will never get financial stability and will live a mediocre life. But happiness is not measured by money alone. In the end, the wealthy and the poor will die, and everything will be left behind. I'm sure life is so beautiful, and we should hope for the best, whatever the best is for people who search for the true meaning of life."

I learned from the true story of these two boys that life takes us to places we don't have any idea exist. We should be leaders, not followers, to get to the top. According to this story, "Marc and David testified that they rode on the wheels of a cargo train for one hundred and seventeen miles and made it alive." They are true achievers. And for all of us, the ride is unique and different, sometimes very dangerous. Still, it will give us a chance to face the challenges, and it will take us to the end of the tunnel, and eventually, we will see the light.

Hope

Danny Knus sat on the grass at his favorite and usual spot. I chose to stand up to hear his new and interesting story. "Revolori decided to give me a good piece of advice," Knus said. "Perhaps, he had heard it from someone else, or maybe it came deep from his heart right at that moment."

Knus went on, telling me that Revolori said, "Certainly, I'm sure that standing up straight and tall, shoulders back and chin high, we will gain respect, and we will correct our posture. If we put our guard down, we are looking for trouble, and we'll never be able to stand on our feet. If the sky falls down, we should get together to pick it up and put it back in place. The choice is ours. If we train our minds, the results will show in many ways. Life gives us opportunities in equal amounts. From the day we are born, we are free to take our own chances, and we make it happen if we work hard. People become successful because they set their minds to do the work. We should follow their leadership and start now. Tomorrow will be another day. Jesus said, 'Let tomorrow worry about itself, work today for tomorrow; you don't know if it will come.'

"The hope for tomorrow is uncertain, yesterday is gone, but today we can work hard, eat good food, dress with elegance, drink responsibly, and get all the commodities money can buy. We shouldn't wait much longer. We work today, and we'll harvest tomorrow. For instance, if we want to write a book, a screenplay, or a song, let's just grab a pen and start jotting down our ideas. Or if we aspire to become athletes or painters, we must go and get the gear, buy the tools, and give it a shot. We must encourage ourselves and practice all the time. We must invest all the money we have. We mustn't be afraid because soon we'll spend it anyway.

"We should become leaders, not followers, producers, not consumers, and winners, not losers. The beauty of life is hidden in the dark, and it's up to us to bring it back to existence for every mortal to enjoy it. We tot think about how much money we can pile up. Of course, we need enough cash to pay our bills, and to have a better life, but we don't have to go to extremes to get it. We must not be hungry for money and kill for cash. Yes, money talks, my friend, that's true, but it cannot beat or buy death. It is better to be honest and poor than to have all the dough in the world and have a bitter heart. I love deep pockets, and I dream of being a millionaire; there's nothing wrong with that. I work hard—yes, I do—but I enjoy every minute of my life with or without a buck in my pocket. 'For the love of money is the root of all evil.' (1 Timothy 6:10). I'm confident that one day, I will be wealthy enough, but that's just an optimism to anticipate myself for the future.

"I tell you, if we train our brains well, we'll have commodities as we wish. If we master our courage, and we don't let our faith vanish, we'll reap rewards. We came to this world to live and enjoy life, to sow a seed, and to leave a legacy of love and respect. We are no less than the most wealthy, prosperous, and famous person in the world but equal in potential. And, as human beings, we live in the same world and share the same goods, products, and supplies that are available on earth. They're available for all of us who want and dare to grasp them. We should venture and challenge ourselves to become rich, not just in material possessions, but in spiritual enhancement to see what our purpose to be here is, to find the true meaning of life on this enchanted and gorgeous planet called Earth.

"Nevertheless, what's available to us doesn't move in harmony by our thoughts and ideas. The ingredients that spark the creation of new objects are there to be cultivated and crafted by our hands. The inventions happen because we dare to put our ideas together, and we hope that these ideas one day are going to become visible and palpable materials.

This time Revolori went back to his childhood and said, "I was ten years old, and I was walking on a muddy road, in the middle of nowhere. This was a special day, and I was on the way to school. I was daydreaming, I stopped, and I stared for a few seconds to the back of my right hand. I saw an electronic device attached to my hand; of course, it was my imagination sending signals to my brain. I saw images and faces of people talking to me from every corner of the world on the screen window of my invisible device wrapped around my wrist. I kept these events in my memory. I didn't have a soul to tell the awesome ideas that my mind was putting together. Now thirty years later, all my ideas have come true. Someone somewhere had the same idea and created cellphones, and from there, the world has developed—Skype, YouTube, Facebook, Google, to mention a few."

"The hope is alive in my mind. All I need is commitment to put my ideas to work and do what it takes to guide my thoughts. I have to be positive, and the next day it will come to bear the fruits of that, I'm sure. Nowadays, everything is so easy to find, but if we just sit on our buttocks all day long, playing video games or watching worthless videos on YouTube, we will not have an individual advance.

"So, let's hope for a better world. We all should wake up and pray for a new tomorrow. We must dig in the darkness, if we have darkness, and soon we'll get to the other side to reach our final destination. And we'll enjoy all the rewards that come with success." Knus paused, then added me, "Revolori said, 'That's the end,'" Knus told me, "But I will never stop telling you the adventures Revolori told me." Sometimes, I think he was making up his stories, but boy, it was fun to listen to him. Next week, we'll enjoy one more story from our awesome friend, B. M. Revolori.

Faith

This time Knus started his next story slowly, explaining how Revolori began to tell him about his most recent adventure: "I'm not a religious individual, but my faith is solid as a rock. And I glorify God the Creator of the universe. I believe in Jesus Christ as my Lord and personal savior. I know deep in my heart that he's the Son of God, and he gives me peace, love, and truth." He continued, "I respect any kind or form of religion, as long as people are happy, and they seek goodness in the spirit and the flesh. To me, going to church is a good form of praising the Lord, and I know that it brings spiritual connections between brothers and sisters who love to mingle and gather together. Personally, I don't go to church. I choose to praise and talk to the Lord in a closed room, all by myself, in the middle of the night. I also feel the need of my spirit to communicate with the Lord. When I'm eating, I'm working, I'm exercising; in fact, every minute of my life I love to pray. But I don't have to attend any church service.

"Many religious leaders who are my friends have tried to convince me that the only way to get to heaven is by going to church and spending time with other churchgoers. When Catholics come to me, I give them the best welcome I can offer. I sit and chat for as long as they want. I love to listen very patiently, and at the end of our conversation, I look at them and watch their facial expressions. They surely think they have already convinced me to become an active Catholic.

"But my best story I have to tell you about religious leaders is from a Christian minister. A pastor approached me one afternoon while I was detailing my car in the driveway. He greeted me and raised his Bible with pride. I welcomed him, and we sat in between three tall palm trees in the front yard. His initial question was, 'Do you have a Bible?' It took me a few beats to respond with a smile, and I answered him with a question. 'What do you think?' He smiled back and gave me a look.

He started his sermon. 'You see, I grew up a Catholic in Los Angeles. At twenty-seven years of age, I became an atheist. I can give you the reasons, but for now, I'll tell you that salvation came to me five years ago when I got saved. I bring the good news of our Lord Jesus Christ for you, because he's chosen you. He talked to me last night and told me to come to you.' He yelled, 'Hallelujah, praise the Lord.'

"I acknowledged him with a small grin. He wanted to continue preaching to me, but I put a stop to him. I pointed with my index finger to the beat-up car I was cleaning before he arrived. I took a few steps to the car; he remained sitting on the grass. I grabbed three books from the car and came back to the stubborn preacher. I showed him the three books that I was holding up. It was the Bible, the Mormon Book, and the Quran. I proudly spoke up, telling him that I had read each one a couple of times. 'I'm not interested in religion right now, but if I change my mind, you'll be the one I'll call, and I'll join your congregation,' I told him in a loving but convincing voice.

"Faithfully, I must add that we have to have the vision to set our goals to discover the unknown. And faith plays an important role in breaking down the emotional walls around our hearts as we learn to trust in God.

"We have to trust, to respect, to listen to people and to learn from their speeches. Faith is a gift from God. We all receive this skill from the moment we open our eyes to the time we end our physical life and enter to God's paradise or hellfire, where all of us have to end up one day. We are so delicate and wash our physical bodies, but we forget to purify our inner most essence – our soul, spirit, heart, and brain. All the time, physical activities take most of our energy and time. We run back and forth to get control of material things that our hands can touch, and our eyes can see, but we do not worry about taking care of the inside part of us that we can't see. We must start taking care of our inner body, so when we turn to dust and our spirit moves out and goes away, then for eternity we'll get our reward. We tend to forget that we have to feed the spirit as much as we put food in our mouths to keep the balance that will bring us health in the spirit and in the flesh.

"Doctors and scientists worry about selling corporeal health at high prices, and we fall into the traps that they set for us. Patients are brainwashed, they say, 'I'm exercising because my doctor told me to.' We hear people talking among themselves when they are jogging at the parks and walking on the streets. We don't want to take responsibility ourselves; we know as well as doctors that walking is good for our health. "I'm not eating red meat," others explain, "because my doctor ordered me not to eat it." Our body sends us signals when we are eating bad food; we do not need a doctor's orders to eat healthily. Yes, we have to listen to health professionals when we need their help. They are trained professionals who give us medicine to heal faster and get better when we are sick. Faithfully, I believe that if I trust in God and I have faith, I can solve most of my physical and spiritual problems, and if I can, anybody can."

My Way: Helping Hand

My friend Knus began Revolori's adventure. In a previous story, he had mentioned a girl that Benjamin Matthew Revolori had met. He was pleased to give more details as Revolori had narrated it to him, saying that Revolori bit his lower lip, then said, "She was introduced to me, and right on the spot I questioned her to get information. I saw the spark in her eyes. She pleaded with her body language to start a close dad-and-daughter relationship with her, and she said, 'Please don't leave me.' I was lacking the love of a daughter. I had three sons who had moved out with their mother after a cruel and painful divorce that I was still going through. She was sweet, and she had an angelical beautiful soul and body; she immediately filled my heart with pure and endless love.

"I was dating her mother, and she became part of my new family—a very stable one, I have to say.

"With them by my side, I was the happiest man on earth. I had found true love that I never had during the fourteen years of my previous marriage. This sweet and beautiful girl spoke with the voice of a million angels. She was my friend, my little sister, and my angel. I could talk to her better than any other people I knew. I started to help her with her school homework, and with her extracurricular activities. I taught her music, acting, sports, and arts.

"Every morning and every afternoon, she and I used to go running. We took three laps around the block jogging, and three laps walking and talking—that was our routine. In the afternoon after finishing our walk, we came back home, and she prepared a bowl of yogurt, mixed with a banana, raisins, oats, grapes, and she added a spoonful of honey to it. Indeed, she took care of my health.

"She reminded me every single day in the morning and at night to pray. We took turns to lead the prayer, to give thanks to the Lord, and to read the Bible. Many times, I asked myself this question: How can a young girl give me so much love? Truly, I didn't find the answer to my own question. All I can say is, she was my spiritual leader, a good reason for me to live happily, and enjoy every task I took. To me there's nothing more precious than to have a friend, especially if that friend was my daughter. She provided me with unconditional love, respect, and she believed in me. I could rest my head on her shoulder and trust my secrets to my precious little one. My dear daughter was always by my side, helping me. She brought me happiness, and she gave me moral support. I cherished every moment I spent with her. Truly, she gave me the strength to move forward with my life.

"When I was really down, she lifted my energy up and boosted my strength by giving me spiritual support. And she gave me true happiness because she got excellent grades all the time. She started all her personal notes with a special sentence: *To the best dad ever.*

"One time, I was having a conversation with my wife about health issues. I told her to take care of herself because she was gaining some extra pounds. 'If you don't take care of yourself, who will?' I warned her. 'If I don't eat healthily, no one will do it for me,' I concluded. My daughter, who was sitting in the middle, looked at me with the most sincere eyes that I've seen in my entire life. She smiled and said, 'Dad, I will make sure you eat healthily, and I will take care of you always and forever, a pinky promise.' She gave me a thumbs-up. Her mother gave her a smile. I couldn't think about anything but getting up off the chair to bring her right into my arms for a very long time. I wept on her shoulder. I knew right at that moment that it was pure love coming from my daughter's heart. She made me the happiest man in the universe.

"The friendship and love I shared with my daughter on a daily basis was unique, pure, and honest. I wouldn't give it up for all the wealth in the world. I had to admit, happiness had knocked at my door, I opened it, and that joy was staying with me for the rest of my life. I had found my angel; I had a daughter who gave me endless love."

Dreams

"Not too long ago, a seventeen-year-old boy, a dear friend of mine, came to me with no place to hide, and nowhere to run," I'm telling you another true story of our hero, B. M. Revolori, Knus continued with sadness in his broken heart. He said, Revolori told him, "the kid called me on the phone, and asked me if I could see him at once. He lived very close to my office and he took a walk to my place. Twenty-five minutes later, we were sitting and eating Chinese food at Shanghai Restaurant in Anaheim, a place he picked on the way to meet me. He was shaking unstoppably. I tried to calm him down, and I gave him a few mental and physical exercises to control his stress.

"I waited for him to tell me his troubles. I was desperate to hear what this young boy had to say to me. But I didn't want to bother him with questions. It was a long silence as I remained sitting in front of him. He continued cracking his fingers. I grabbed my paper cup filled with water. He stared at me, and picked up his soda pop paper cup too. I started to draw lines on the cup with my index nail. I waited for him to open his mouth and let me know what was bothering him.

"Several minutes went by, and the food was almost gone, but he still gave no sign that he wanted to share anything with me yet. I had known this handsome and talented lad since he was born. I had never seen him as worried as he was that time. I was sad and worried about his health. But I never gave up hope that I was going to be able to help him once he flipped his tongue to tell me about his troubles and doubts.

"Finally, he spoke. 'I trust you, Mr. Revolori,' he said, looking at me with his gorgeous big black eyes rolling. He asked me, 'Have you ever trusted someone once in your life?' I kept my cool for a second. I was silent, and I was still making crazy marks on the white Styrofoam cup.

"Then, I raised my chin up and nodded. He insisted on hearing my answer, and he asked me again. 'Have you ever trusted somebody?' I knew this moment that he wanted me to give him an answer. So, I took a big breath and said, 'Yeah! Yes, I have son, but I was lost in space for a second.'

'You see,' he said, 'I had a dream – the same dream for three consecutive nights. I know this dream will come true, and I also know what it means already. This is what I dreamed: I saw myself walking in a hilly field of tall green grass. I saw a tree covered with oranges. The branches were hanging lower, almost kissing the ground. Some of them were already broken because the weight of the oranges was too much. I saw a multitude of people coming from around the world. They were coming to eat its fruit, and to rest underneath, for its shade was abundant and majestically covered one quarter of the earth. Soon, I realized that I was the tree where people came to rest and to eat. My father had planted that tree some years back. He made sure to water it every morning and every afternoon. He planted three trees in total: an olive tree, a fig tree, and the orange tree. But he took very special care of the orange tree. Three men in black came by, and they told me to go with them and leave my dad alone forever. They signed a contract with me. They promised me they were going to make me the best, the wealthiest, and most powerful man in the world, if I stayed with them. My dad had asked me to work with him in the small family business we owned. Dad became disappointed, and he went away with tears streaming down his wrinkled face. He planted another orange tree that same day. The tree produced and ripened oranges right away and fed half of the people of the earth. I dreamed the same dream two times every night, for three nights. I couldn't sleep for the rest of the week. I tried to put my thoughts together for two days, to find a way to tell my dad what I had dreamed. I didn't know how he was going to take it and to react.

'Eventually, I made my mind up and called my dad. I asked him if he would like to have a meeting with me, for my dad was a busy man, but he always found time to be with my brothers and me. I told him the dream, and I gave him my own interpretation right away. He listened to me, then as always, he answered me with authority, and he told me that he wanted me to wait for a few days, and we would have the right answer. I insisted that my interpretation was right, he said, 'You might be right, but we must wait. God works in mysterious ways. Just be patient, don't rush it.'

"Three days later, early in the morning, I received a text message from him. The text read: 'I love you, bro, and I'm proud of you.' My dad used to call me brother as far as I can remember.

The same day at noontime, he was driving down Lincoln Avenue a busy street. He was taking me back home. In a few minutes, we arrived at my apartment complex. He pulled to the side and parked for a few minutes. I was opening the door to get off, but my dad tiredly spoke. 'I already have the answer, and I know the interpretation for your dream. I went back to the seat and closed the door. My dad spoke calmly. 'I also had a dream last night,' he said, 'I was pacing back and forth in the dark, I was walking through big corridors of this huge mansion I owned. A young man was sitting on a metal bench. He was hiding his face in the dark so I could not recognize him, but he had the look of an angel watching out for me. He stared at me all the time, and he approved my movements with a unique nod. A blonde lady showed her face through the main door. She walked directly toward me at a fast pace. A whole family of Mexicans led by Rudolph Camillo entered. Camillo started to congratulate me with a loud voice. In fact, the Mexican guy spoke to me without giving me time to give him the okay to do so. His wife followed him nodding, and his son was behind them. Mr. Camillo kept talking and yelling, then he said, 'My wife told me how famous your son became with the release of his new movie. I'm here to make you an offer you can't resist. I want to represent him, and I will pay you twenty-four dollars a day, and I'll give you a short-term contract of three years. Here is the contract, sign it right now.' I was quiet for a moment, but he bugged me so much that he annoyed the young man on the bench. He got up to confront him, and he explained to Camillo that he had made me an offer of three thousand dollars a day, and that I had already signed the contract with him. The Mexican family stepped out, and I also saw the blonde lady disappearing in the distance without saying a word. I turned to the bench, and the angel was still giving me a thumbs-up. I walked towards him and saw his whole body for the first time. His face was bright and constantly changing colors. He got up to turn around and went his way. I stayed for a little longer still pacing back and forth."

"My dad finished telling me his dream. And he added, 'Now, you got the true meaning of your dream. Your own interpretation is incorrect.' He started the engine up, and he motioned me with a facial expression to step out of his car.

"I did not pay attention to my dad, and I did what I thought was the right thing to do. I made a big mistake because that was the last time I've ever seen or spoken with him."

Revolori sighed, and he admitted that he was sure this boy had made the worst mistake of his life. He had been very close to his dad, who cared so much for him. They were brothers for God's sake. Now he has lost his father for good. I was shocked to hear the story' I was sad to know that this young man got in trouble and ended up without a father figure to care for him. Revolori broke into tears, and sadly he said, "I was unable to help or save him." I tried to find the words to encourage him, but none came to my mind. I just stared at him while he was ending this sad story.

Revolori concluded, "I did not know what to do to help this kid mend the problem. I advised him to call his father to apologize. It was all I could think to offer him. Surely, he was wrong, but his dad would forgive him, and of that I was sure." Sometimes the errors we make are so severe that we have to live in misery for the rest of our lives. Many times we don't learn the lesson, but I hope this young boy finds peace in his heart wherever he is. Nevertheless, he might have to wait for a long time to cure his suffering, or he'll never find peace to stop the pain. Life's rough and tough. When teenagers think they know everything they'll lose it all in the blink of an eye." Revolori took off his glasses, still sobbing.

The Challenge

Knus started his once-a-week tale while he was holding two cans of energizer drinks in his hands. Revolori had shared this story, Knus said: "A man got married, and five years later he was the proud father of two sons. They grew up in a healthy environment. Pops was very dedicated to the boys. He didn't take much care of himself the only gift he gave himself was the very basics for a modest living. He spent a fortune in sports coaching, music lessons, art classes, and academic education for the boys. His sons went to the best private elementary and secondary schools he could afford. In fact, he gave them whatever they asked him for. He purchased them educational toys, books, games, software, computers, and other things they wanted and needed. He had so much faith in them, and every so often he introduced them to his friends and humbly he showed off his boys' talents.

"From the time they were born, he hired professional child caregivers. At six and five years of age, he chose nicknames for the boys: The older boy's nickname was Mitto. He had great talent in music. At that age, he showed great abilities playing the guitar, drums, bass, and piano. He also received an extensive coaching in acting and singing. Verdo, the younger son, didn't do so well; he just followed what his brother was doing for he was lazy. Mitto was very obedient and made Dad proud and happy. They grew up fast, and they became in love with sports. They practiced soccer, basketball, baseball, and they registered for golf instructions at the Tiger Woods Teaching Center at Dad Miller in Anaheim. They spent most of their free time enjoying and playing recreational soccer. Soon they signed up to top competitive soccer clubs. Mitto had the skills and the talents, and Verdo had confidence, discipline, and stamina. They both had a successful life in sports. They wanted to go pro, but their dad knew it wasn't possible because they didn't have what it took; nonetheless, he supported them and encouraged to pursue their dreams. He was always there supporting them both financially, and giving them moral guidance to go for their goals. They had the tools, the coaches, and the equipment to train hard. Their mother wasn't in the picture at all. She enjoyed life her own way. The man was determined to make his sons successful. He spent hours talking to them about the principles of civilization. He taught them how some people can become wealthy overnight. He gave them names of people who made history coming from nothing, and the boys became very knowledgeable. They listened to him at first with admiration and interest, but later on when peer pressure became a factor in their lives, they disobeyed and criticized him drastically.

"He knew he was losing them, but he never gave up his dream to make them winners. And that hope kept the flame burning in his heart. He made his mind up and went the extra mile to make his boys leaders and not followers.

"He spent a lot of time lecturing Mitto and Verdo about the toughness of life. He taught them the easy ways to handle every single problem. He showed them some tips to solve any adversity and provided tools to win the most dangerous battles. He opened their minds, for them to go forward and to take the right path. In abundance, he gave them for free, for he believed he had received free true gifts of God in Christ.

When Mitto was nine years old and Verdo was eight, they were walking to the office. Mitto was complaining about the long walk. He asked, 'Dad, why are we walking? You shouldn't have let Mom take the car. I don't want to walk, it's so hot and I am already tired.' Mitto complained over and over again. His dad took it easy for a moment, but then he reacted and gave Mitto the lesson of his life. It was going to be a learning punishment for Mitto. Suddenly, his dad yelled, 'Sit down!' Mitto did as his dad ordered him. Verdo watched, and he stood on the sidewalk edge. The man took his eyes off Mitto for a moment and gave Verdo a scary look. 'Take off your shoes,' he commanded in a military fashion. Mitto's eyes started to water; he didn't understand what was going on. Mitto was very angry. 'Take off your shoes,' his dad said a second time. Mitto followed his instructions to the letter. 'Your socks! They have to come off too,' the dad added in a loud voice. The sun was shining as bright as you could expect on that hot summer day. The pavement was baked; sons and dad were sweating all over their bodies. Mitto got up from the edge of the sidewalk as soon as he heard the roar and the word, *'Up!'* A second of silence came, and then his dad yelled, *'Walk!'* Mitto took a few steps barefoot; he immediately jumped on his tiptoes and begged his pops to stop. Dad grabbed him, held him to his chest, and carried him in his arms and went to the shade under a tree. He helped him put his socks and shoes back on.

"The dad went on, 'Son, what I did to you right now is teach you a lesson, and you, Verdo, listen and listen good to what I have to say. There are children around the world who walk miles barefoot because they cannot afford a single pair of shoes, not even rubber boots. You have fancy tennis shoes. You are Americans, you have cars, expensive toys, games, bicycles, and all that money can buy, and you are complaining just because you have to walk to the office, a fifteen-minute walk.' The man said, "The truth? I walked without shoes every single day for the first twelve year of my life, because my dad couldn't afford to buy me a pair of shoes. That attitude is not acceptable. Shame on you,' he ended.

"They learned their lesson. A month later, the old man and the boys were taking a longer walk to work at a different office. They were crossing the 5 Freeway on Euclid Avenue in the city of Anaheim. Mitto stopped in the middle of the freeway bridge, and smiling told his dad, 'Pops, I learned the lesson, and I'm happy to walk. Besides, walking is good for your health. Right? Or at least I hear doctors say that on TV commercials.'

"This is a special story that shows that we parents need to choose the right approach to discipline our children. We need to use the best programs available to discipline and educate our kids. For example, the balance of punishment and love is a good tool in the raising of teenagers. It is necessary, and it has to be applied to provide security and respect. Governments, schools, public and private institutions that have programs to educate children should teach them a variety of methods, and not just the conventional way. Some parents fear that they are going to lose their children or get in trouble with social services or any office that provides safety for children if they give tough discipline to their children.

"But, at the end of the day, we parents should make the decision on how to educate and raise our children. The tools are there sealed in our hearts from birth; no parent lacks the natural ability to raise children well. The only problem, I see, is that we provide too much love, but we don't stop to think that we need to punish them for their bad behavior too. Because love is passion, a feeling that comes from the heart, but caring is spending extra time with them, helping them with all their homework, activities, and work with their discipline each day. We should punish them one way or another for their wrongdoings, and reward them for the excellent reports and good behavior we get from them." Revolori looked up and said, "Let's raise kids well, and we'll make them leaders."

Catch of the Day

This is was a favorite story that Revolori shared with Knus, he told me. A true story of three boys. "The first son decided to leave his father at the age of seventeen, the second at fifteen, and a fourteen-month-old baby boy didn't have a choice but to go with Mommy and his brothers. He couldn't choose to go or stay, he had to leave his dad.

"The playground had just welcomed this cute innocent infant. I cannot understand how we go to school and get sophisticated trainings and study mathematics, architecture, science, and many other subjects and programs offered at all universities around the world. But with all the knowledge we achieve, we don't have compassion for our children, and we take away their happiness. Many times, it's the father who takes the first step to abandon them, some other times the mother is the one who cares less for them. Children don't know what's going on either way, and the only thing they're sure of is that they need care from both parents. They cry and no one listens to them; nobody approaches to calm them down. Why don't we fall on our knees to pray for forgiveness and ask God to help us how to raise them well? We must make sure to give them true happiness.

"Understanding the reason why we came to this beautiful paradise is easy but taking responsibility to make our wonderful small world a better place for everybody is not that much fun. We struggle to pile up money, and it makes us all greedy and aggressive, and we are money hungry and hope to get all the material possessions we can. But, if we'll spend twenty minutes a day to share our love, our wisdom, and to teach children good activities, in time they will enjoy a successful life. We have to give quality time to listen to them, try to understand them, and help them to solve their problems, and then the world will definitely be a beautiful, better, and a safer place to live.

"Divorcing parents are increasing, and no one is taking any responsibility to find a solution to reduce that negative high percentage of divorcing parents. Couples who are divorcing all over the world seek legal help with attorneys to end their marriages, but they do not understand that the best way is to talk it over with their spouses and reach an agreement that benefits themselves. Lawyers should be hired as a last resource. They are not just throwing money in the trash paying high legal fees, but ruining their lives, and tearing their children apart. It is hard to understand and to accept that life is not to be wasted away, but for families to live in harmony, where spouses and children enjoy a happy and healthy family life together.

"When the thoughts of separations come to knock on the door, we must close it and lock it up for good. I went through a nasty divorce that ruined my life. It hurt me a great deal, but my three children suffered the most, emotionally and physically, because they couldn't play with me anymore all the time they wanted. They were thrown out in a hostile world before the time was right for them to stand on their feet alone. They didn't know how painfuhat would be. I remember when my ex-wife told me she didn't want to live with me anymore, and I asked her why. She answered, asking me a weird question. This is what she asked me: 'Give me ten good reasons why I shouldn't split?' On the double, I gave her two, the first answer was: 'What about our children? Surely, we need to raise them?' And the second one was: 'What about our fifteen years of marriage?' Two answers weren't enough for her. She said, 'I expected ten not two, and I don't have any to give you.' And that was the end of my marriage. Of course, I spent the next ten months trying to convince her to think it over, and I hoped we'd reach an agreement to get back together. But she didn't want to hear me out, and every day we sank deeper, and at the end we fell apart.

"At the beginning, our children were very supportive. They shared time with both of us and didn't favor their mother or me. All things were coming along as planned, but time went by fast, and I filed for divorce with the Superior Court of California, county of Orange. Then everything turned around, and the trouble started. I was visiting my children every single day; in fact, I was taking care of them all day long, and I was very happy to do that. The day the divorce papers were served, my visiting days were reduced to the weekends only. And when the judgment was signed, my visiting times were none. I was devastated; I did not know what to do or where to go. In spite of that, I found a way to visit them once in a while for the next six months. One day, my oldest son, who was seventeen, stopped talking to me. My middle son promised me he wasn't going to leave me; I had at least one son to lean on, I thought. Not for long, though. He turned eighteen, and I took him to eat out to celebrate his birthday. We had a great last time together. The time had gone very quickly. He had a lovely birthday lunch with my two-year-old baby son and me at Lucile's BBQ, his favorite restaurant, in the city of Brea. I was so happy, and we made plans for the future. Unfortunately, the plans didn't last long.

"The next day, I received a text message from him. He wanted me to read an email he had just sent me. It was about ten at night, and I was getting ready to go to bed. I had a terrifying feeling when I saw the text. My thought was this question: *Is it good or bad news?* I knew that it was a bad piece of news because my brain sent the sad message to my achy broken heart before I read the email.

"The email said, 'I already turned eighteen, bro, and I am a free man now. I'm going to start from scratch, and it is time for you to step down. But I'll visit you once in a while.' I was very sad, but being a strong, spiritual individual, I composed myself and called him back as he had asked me to do it. As soon as he answered, he asked me, 'What do you think about the email, bro?' I took a big breath and answered, 'Don't worry about it, everything is okay.'

"I met with him the next day, and we had a conversation about our business. The meeting was very brief. We made an appointment to meet again the next day, to bring the contract bank statements to our last meeting. I drove to the nearest Chase Bank to get the statements and to withdraw the balance we had of $36,000 to split – $24,000 for him and $12,000 for me. We met a second time the next morning at the same place. We had met last, at a McDonald's in Van Nuys. We were still missing some very important court order papers, so we set a third meeting. This time we had to do it at a Chase Bank location. The third day came, and in about ten minutes it was all over. That was the last time we saw or talked to each other."

Fear of Flying

That day, as I was walking in the driveway, Knus told me he had a good story for me. He followed me, and he was almost screaming with his thunderous voice. "This is what happened to me," Revolori said. "Miraculously, I got rid of my fear of flying after the death of my younger brother, Hannibal," Revolori continued. "And now, I'm not afraid of flying anymore." The story went like this: "My three sons and I were going to Charlotte from LAX. We made a quick stop in Atlanta. My kids and I came to the lobby to wait for the connecting flight to Charlotte. We sat for forty-five minutes waiting to board at gate 22. Ben sat on my lap." Knus told me this story with a lot of excitement. After a long pause, Knus continued, "And Revolori said, 'I was shivering uncontrollably, for I had a deathly fear of flying. My sons were listening to music and playing games on their cell phones. My little baby was sleeping, and I kept massaging his head very gently.

"Two hours later, we walked to the boarding gate, and into the aircraft we went. We got on the plane and took our seats. Ben was sitting with my older son sharing the same seat. I sat and rested the back of my head on the top of the reclining seat. I didn't move an inch. My older son tried to encourage me to relax, but I was glued to the seat, motionless and silent. Every minute that passed by, I was attached to the seat, thinking about the takeoff and the landing. All the passengers sat down, and I opened my eyes to take a look, then closed them immediately. I was very frightened, and I was having a hard time breathing. I started praying in my mind. I stretched out my left arm and placed it on the tiny legs of my baby boy, but I still kept my eyes closed.

"The flight attendants began to prepare the crew and passengers for takeoff. The pilot addressed the passengers, and the monitors were turned on for the safety procedures. The aircraft was pulled back out of the gate to the runway.

"Suddenly, I felt a moment of peace. I didn't know what was happening, but magically my fear of flying was gone. I smiled and pinched my cheeks. The plane took off and rocketed up straight into the blue sky. It never stopped to level off. I turned to my sons with a grin and with my eyes still closed. I was sure—or at least my mind told me—that we were going all the way up to reach the stars. I took a deep breath when the majestic eagle spread its wings and rolled over several times.

"Finally, the plane went down to its altitude. The captain addressed the passengers again. I came back to reality and opened my eyes. Now I realized that all had been an illusion, but my heart was beating fast, and I knew deep inside that something was going wrong. I tried to come up with an interpretation, and I didn't even remember that I was still up in the air. My phobia of heights was gone. I was still having a long conversation with myself, and I didn't know that the plane was already landing. The flight attendant ran to my seat to tell me that I needed to put my seat upright. I did as she asked me, and she went back to take a seat for the plane was about to touch the ground.

"A few minutes later, the aircraft was taxiing to the gate. Passengers were reaching up and grabbing bags, suitcases, and all kind of items from the overhead compartments. I stayed in my seat, my seatbelt still fastened. Almost all the passengers had exited, and my sons were going out the long aisle. I looked at them and raised one hand for them to slow down and wait for me. They walked through the exit door and went out the tunnel. They stopped at the waiting room. Then they moved down to the carousel to pick up our luggage. David, the son of the executive producer, escorted us to the bus, which would take us to our hotel.

"We were still on the bus when my cell phone rang. I picked the call up and answered, hearing a female voice crying, saying, 'Your brother, Hannibal, is dead. I'm sorry to tell you the sad news, honey.' Calmly, I listened, and with a big smile from ear to ear, I answered her, 'I already know it.' 'What do you mean?' my wife asked. I paused. Yes, I already knew it. Joyfully, I replied to her, 'An angel came to the plane and told me.'

"Happily, I chuckled and sighed, a couple of tears trickled down my left cheek. I closed my cell phone, and turned to the left. I stretched my left arm to rest it on the window edge trim. I stared up to the sky, and I spotted a single cloud dancing alone in the middle of the sky. I got my phone ready to shoot a video, and in a matter of seconds the cloud moved closer to me. I waved at it, and in a soft voice, my brother spoke to me from the cloud. Clearly, I heard the words that told me, 'Call me.'

"We arrived at the hotel at about eight in the evening. The boys were tired and got into bed immediately. We had two suites connected to each other. Ben was sleeping like an angel, my older son was snorting in a minute, and my middle son was complaining of a headache. I gave him a glass of water and a painkiller. Then, I went to my room, where Ben was sleeping. After checking and making sure my older sons were safe, I walked to my bed and sat next to Ben.

"I grabbed a Bible from the drawer and read it for a few minutes, then I said my prayers and I went to sleep. Suddenly, I heard a knock on my room door. I got up and opened it; nobody was there. I went back to sleep, and again someone was knocking on the door. I went back to open it a second time, but I didn't see anyone. I came back and hit the sack a third time. A call and a knock were coming from the door once again. This time, with a sweet and soft voice, I answered from the bed. Then I went to the door to open it one last time. Ten seconds after, I had taken a look from the bed. The door opened by itself before I grabbed the doorknob. I saw a figure standing and holding the doorknob. He was hiding his face; I just stood there and listened to what he told me.

"My brother, Hannibal, started telling me slowly, 'I'm taking away all your fears and phobias. You won't be afraid of flying anymore; your fear of darkness is also gone. I died, but I am freeing you from all the junk that has bothered you and has made your life miserable since you were a baby.' A second time he said, 'Call me.' I was about to ask questions, but it was too late. My brother had vanished in the darkness. Three months later, I wrote, 'Call me.'" Revolori said, "It was a special song dedicated to him."

Searching for the Unknown

"This one is from my own personal experience," Revolori told me. "Today I am sharing my successful secrets," he continued. "I always try to learn more than what I already know. Every breath I take, I try to use it wisely searching for new opportunities. It's like food in my mouth, and it tastes yummy. This way I find new things unknown to me ready to be discovered. I just think about what I have to do, and I stretch my hand out to grasp it. My mind never comes to a stop during the day or at night. I think all the time to ask questions of others and even of myself. At times, I come up with answers my own way or I make them up to have a little fun. Every dream I have is a new challenge for me. I don't give up until I come up with an interpretation, whether it is good or bad, positive or negative. I challenge myself to the best of my abilities; I give strength to my mind and my spirit when I am down. For me, thinking is an endless journey. I always put up a good fight, and at the end of the day, whether I win or lose, I'm happy with the outcome. I take the risks every single day, and my challenge continues forever.

"I believe every man in the world has the ability to create. The brain is a sharp computer that, if we use it properly, it will bring productive results. On the other hand, if we mess with it or if we train it with irrational intention, it will destroy us. The most sophisticated machines or lethal weapons are operated and programed by men, and by themselves they are not dangerous. So, we can be sure that without human involvement, every piece of equipment would sit inactive. To understand better the power of humans, we just need to sit down, relax, and think with no worries, and let our imagination take us to the unknown. Then we come back out with energy and new ideas to make changes in the future and bring more knowledge to ourselves. The next step is to work hard with those ideas that come to our minds. We polish them, review them, and hopefully we will make it happen. Once they give us products and goods, we put them in the hands of wise businessmen so the whole world can benefit from them.

"Certainly, it's almost impossible to keep good inventions out of the reach of crazy people who want to make an extra penny out of them, no matter who they have to hurt in the process. They don't hesitate to kill to accomplish their goals. At this point, there is nothing the inventor can do but hope and pray for the best. Creators can only dream that their inventions serve the needy, and they hope that every person in the world gets a piece of the pie.

"In my lifetime, I have taken the challenges. I strongly believe in taking risks and working hard, not with what is already out, but with things that are hidden somewhere in the universe. I know deep in my soul that God will reveal hidden things to those who ask and are willing to take the extra step and go the extra mile to make new discoveries. I heard singer-songwriter Paul Simon answering a question about songwriting. He said, 'Songs are already there. All we have to do is fix them up and cut them.'

"I teach children for free in my own time so they learn to dream, to work hard, and to set their minds to follow their dreams. A few of them respond very well, and they think about being producers, becoming winners, and to be leaders in this world that we live in.

"I used to have a close friendship with an actress miles away. She lived in Europe, and I communicated with her on the phone. She used to call me twice a week. She always shared with me almost everything that she was going through. I knew a lot about her family, her dreams, and her marital relationship. One day she told me, 'I want to talk about my seven-year-old daughter.' I took a long pause; I thought she was going to ask me to help her financially. She continued speaking with a steady voice. 'My daughter has a very high IQ. She's special. I know because I can't stop her from saying what's on her mind.' Of course, I thought twice to cut her off and to tell her what my true answer was. She asked, 'What's your take on that?' And my response was: 'That's what all parents say about their children.' 'No,' she said, interrupting me, 'I'm telling you the truth. If you want to believe me, fine; if you don't, it's great too.'

"Two years passed. I kept in touch with her, and our communication remained as good as it had been from the first time we spoke. As a matter of fact, I was her spiritual leader, her financial advisor, and her talent manager. She told me what she did, whether it was good or bad. She shared with me almost everything.

"Once, she came to Los Angeles to audition for the Brogan Talent Agency, and she introduced me to her daughter in person. The girl was already nine years old. She spent three weeks with me, enough time to learn about her IQ. Her daughter and I became best friends and we talked for hours. I remembered what her mother had told me about her IQ. I took the opportunity to test her. It was easy for me for I had already bonded with her and she trusted me. I asked her if she could play any musical instrument, and she answered no. I went on to ask if she wanted to learn singing and playing the piano. She opened her eyes wide and nodded.

"Immediately, I started coaching her, and in a couple of lessons she knew how to play all the chords that I had taught her. I gave her a few voice lessons, and she was almost pitch-perfect, and with my help she wrote her first song. For sure, she impressed me because she didn't know how to speak English, and she was learning way better than many of the English-speaking students.

"She was the best speller that I'd ever met in my entire life. I gave her easy words to spell, and she spelled them so fast. I thought, *How in the world does she do it if she's not knowledgeable in English grammar, and she is not a native English speaker?* I gave her big words. This was a challenge, I thought, she wouldn't be able to handle. But she got all of them right. I decided to test her honesty. I'd been picking big words and phrases from the signs because I was driving on the San Pedro Freeway. I stopped reading words from the signs, and I gave her the words 'conventional' and 'fictitious' to spell. I got them from the top of my head. She told me she couldn't spell these because the ones I gave her before she had read from the signs. There it was, she was cheating.

"In this day and age, I have found out that we can learn good lessons from everybody, and we must take advantage to enrich our knowledge about human behavior."

Cultural Pride

One of my hobbies is asking people to tell me about their culture. I enjoy learning about cultures and world history. I have had the chance to hear people from many countries around the world telling me their stories. This way, I've learned a lot about their cultural backgrounds. They all have unique lifestyles, and they're very happy to talk about their past and present cultural enrichment. They're proud of their food, their culture, their lifestyles, and the history of their countries of origin. It is important for them to defend their countries of birth and preserve their cultures, even if they are living in America.

Nowadays, people all over the globe can share their history, and they love to talk about true and made-up stories. It's cool for them to spread the word with the new advances in technology. Ancient cultures have been mixing with new ones, and modern cultures can show off the beauty of the new fusion. At present, it's easy to understand the changes of new societies that have emerged around the universe. Nowadays, anyone can upload and download videos, images, and photos on social media. All of this is done with a simple click to enter information on the wide net, and in a blink of an eye they post the photos and videos. Whereas, in the past, to learn true and correct information about other countries, it took a lot of time to search in books, the old way of research is almost gone. Only a few shelves are filled up with old dusty books in a few libraries and bookstores. We know people don't read books as much as they used to, but they sit in front of screens on computers, tablets, and cell phones. They spend much of their free time online. Hardcover or paperback books are almost unavailable. They have been replaced by all kinds of electronic devices. And almost all educational programs we use these days are on computer application software. I'm not saying that this way of learning is bad; I'm just talking about the difference between the two methods of learning about history. Both have their advantages and disadvantages. I don't mind using either one. I get the information that I need either way, and I am happy to utilize the two resources that are available to the public.

One thing I am sure of, now I get information on the double, and I don't have to do research for a long time.

I like online searches to retrieve information fast and easily, but I still go to libraries to read and check out books. I also spend long hours every day in front of the computer screen, punching commands and pressing keys on the keyboard. I'm happy that technology makes everything easy and fast, but I'm concerned that it makes me a little lazy, and I don't have to force my mind to work hard as I did before. I try to take advantage of the moment, and I love to learn a lot about people and their culture.

I have a great knowledge of Western culture (Europe and America), and I know a lot about Eastern culture (China, India, and the Middle East), and I enjoy reading them both. I have also traveled to many countries in Europe (Germany, France, Poland, the Netherlands, Denmark, and others) to mingle among the locals who have lived there for generations. It has been my favorite form of gathering information right from the source. The data that I have gathered in writings and from word of mouth has been passed to them from their ancestors; it is so important to me, because I get it directly from their traditions.

In one of my trips to India, I met a guy named Varun Uppunda. He became a close friend of mine, and he took me many times to exotic places in big cities and small villages. I had the privilege of talking to villagers and going to their mud-plastered homes. Several times I saw how they struggle to survive. They cooked their meals on fires fueled with pieces of wood or dry branches that they cut from dead trees. It was unique that big-horned bulls were resting and munching grass tied to wooden poles inside their owners' rooms. It was amazing how the cows lived with their masters inside their houses; animals and people living in perfect harmony. I asked my friend, Varun to, ask them a few questions in their native language. They started a productive conversation, and they immediately asked Varun if I was from America. When my friend told them that I was an American citizen, they gladly answered all my questions.

I pulled out my camera and started to take pictures, and they asked me to pose with them. I have to mention that this was the most precious moment I have had in my entire trip. From that instant, I felt that my whole body was being injected with a magic potion of love for India, the Indian culture, and their unique lifestyle.

Business Class

I took a plane from Los Angeles to New York City, and after five hours I arrived at the airport, then my fourteen-year-old son and I were taken to a hotel at Times Square. We spent two weeks in New York City; as always, time flies, and the days and the two weeks went by so fast. I didn't realize it was time to head back home. Certainly, we had to go back to join my wife who was waiting for us in LA.

There we were at the airport waiting in line to pass the security screening gates. Some passengers started to complain that we were going through security without delays. The production company had arranged and paid for business class, and everything was included.

When we got on the plane, we were looking for our seats in the business class cabin. Passengers who were already in their seats gave us hostile stares. I made myself comfortable, ignoring the pointed comments and the dirty looks. An Indian passenger stood up and started complaining to the flight attendant. Next to me, a Chinese guy was petting his dog in a fancy cage, and the passengers were paying compliments to the dog and its owner. But they were still giving nasty looks to my son, and even the flight attendants were ignoring us. From the comments, it appeared they didn't believe that we could afford expensive tickets because we were Hispanics. The Chinese fellow stood up, and wiped up his forehead with a red handkerchief.

I must say that he wore everything in red colors. The cage was red, and he was wearing a red long-sleeved shirt and a red tie.

My son got very depressed, and four weeks after the bad flight experience, he still wanted answers. He asked questions in a million ways, but he couldn't hear a satisfactory answer. He couldn't understand the cruelty of people and started to become aggressive. One day, I listened to his complaints, and I promised him that most people are not bad. There are more good souls in this barbaric world than mean human beings. For each bomb that explodes, there are millions of hugs that people give to each other every minute. But one bomb makes more noise than a million hugs. Evil destroys itself, but good deeds help us to solve our differences.

I got up and gave him a big hug. He asked, "What's that for?" I told him, "I'm showing you what love is all about. And it can come with a hug, with a smile, or a word, but not with hate, anger, and mistreatment. Be prepared, young man, to fight evil with goodness, and if you do that, you'll surely inherit the kingdom of heaven, even when you still have your feet in this beautiful and enchanted planet.

"I know you went through a horrible experience on that plane, and they treated us badly. In fact, they treated us worse than the dog in the cage, but that won't make you a loser but a winner. It will put you over the top, and one day, they'll learn to respect you."

After I finished my speech, I shook his hand and gave him a smile. He smiled back at me, and he said, "Thank you, Pops, you're awesome!" He stood tall, kicked the dust, and as he was walking away, he turned back and waved me good-bye. I just raised my hand and saluted him.

Three Stars

I, Danny Knus, started early to mow the lawn. That morning, I was smiling when I saw Mario Revolori-Quinones walking with his head down. He came toward me to meet me halfway. He greeted me with a genuine hello, and he stretched out his arms for a long embrace. It was very unusual because he knew I was a dry, rude, and grotesque man. He laughed to see me still smiling and sticking out my sharp tongue through my missing teeth. I said, "Here's where the story about Revolori that I've been telling you becomes personal, sad, and bloody." I briefed him, "I urge you to pay close attention."

That day I showed up earlier than usual. I was carrying a basket of red flowers to replace the dead plants in the small garden. I started to remove the withered flowers to dig holes and plant the healthy ones; he jumped into his car and started it up. I dropped the small shovel and rushed to the passenger door. He rolled down the window glass for me to rest my elbows on the edge of the door. "What's the hurry today?" I asked. "Don't you have time for a short and interesting chat?" He replied, "I'll be back in a flash, and I'll have the whole day to listen to you." I took a step back and let him drive away.

Minutes later, I sat on a thick log. He was standing; I asked him to sit down. I said, "Today you'll hear a touching and sad story.

"Listen and listen good, Mr. Revolori." I told him that my family and friends call me BDM. It is short for Bad Devil Man. I laughed and told him that I was just kidding. Really, it stands for Best Dreamer Monkey. As you see, I have a distinctive sense of humor. I'm not that mean.

"I have been sharing with you a few boring stories, but today I will go for the golden tale. I promise you're going to love it. It will take me two weeks to finish the whole thing. I ask you to be patient and enjoy it. You won't hear anything like it in your lifetime."

I took a pause, I massaged the back of my head, and I stretched my hands out. I said, "Revolori, you are an interesting fellow. A week ago, you were sleeping with your wife, a gorgeous young lady, and you were playing with your three handsome sons." I stopped to catch my breath. Then, I added, "You have the same last name as my dear friend, Benjamin Matthew Revolori. Listen, you're still enjoying a good financial lifestyle, and everything is going well. I've been your friend since I have started to work for you five years ago. During these years, I know you have had a happy life, and you had an awesome relationship with your family." I put it this way: "You were having a great time.

"You are one of the most extraordinary dads and husbands that I have ever met. But soon your luck will change. Gradually, you'll be standing on the age of a cliff. I know you have a lot of patience, but your sons, your wife, your brothers, and your close friends will persecute you without mercy. Like I already said, you have a lot of patience. I have never seen a person as patient as you. A few days ago, you went inside your bedroom, and you saw your wife kissing and hugging one of your younger brothers. Isn't it true?

"Be aware, your life will take a big turn; you'll not know what to do or how to get back on your feet. It will happen soon. You'll be sleeping in your car for the next six months, and you'll spend all day long at a park." And I continued my conversation, assuring him that I would go to the park and visit him quite often. I added, "I tell you, you'll have my support. You have to trust me, and this is how the real story of your life began forty years back. You have won three stars already. If you survive the next stroke and finish the race, you'll receive your fourth crown, that will be awarded in heaven." Revolori stared at me and shook his head.

First Stroke

I said, "Don't ask me how I know all about your life because I won't say a word. Today is the first time I have decided to talk to you about your personal life story. I brought you three slices of homemade pizza because I know you're allergic to junk food." I cried like a baby to see Mario Revolori-Quinones enjoying his food. I leaned on the wall to ease up my emotions that soon went away. I offered him a soda pop, which he rejected. He said that he hadn't drunk any sweet beverage for a very long time—since he had his first deadly stroke. I interrupted him and took over the story. "Yeah! You were eight when you became a quadriplegic for two years. Now you're allergic to sweeteners, preserved food, and you even have allergies to bottled drinks including bottled water. All you drink is purified water; you even drink tap water, as long as it is fresh.

"You're so blessed. You don't have to spend a lot of money on drinks and packaged foods. The best part is that you eat and drink fresh all the time. But you must admit that sometimes, you crave a cup of hot chocolate or a cup of black coffee. You used to drink it black—no sugar, no cream—back in the good old days; that was the way you swigged it. You haven't been able to eat greasy food since you were eight years old. And now I'm reminding you why you haven't eaten junk food since then. I must say that now you eat only rice, vegetables, and fruit, and drink nothing but water, organic fresh drinks, and freshly squeezed all-fruit juices. And I believe you're not complaining at all. You're happy to be who you are. You love yourself so dearly, and what's cool is you love others, including your enemies. That's right!

"I'm going to be honest with you. I found out that you have taken prescription medicine to control and prevent your allergies, but you haven't been successful. Every time you eat preserved foods, you get insane migraine headaches, a sore throat, and have difficulty breathing.

"Deadly food allergies are good for you because they regulate your eating habits, and you enjoy good health as long as you don't eat them. You are blessed," I told him almost whispering. Revolori nodded. "In some instances, you have been rushed to the hospital in critical condition because you just tried a bite of packaged food or a sip of coffee.

"You suffer deadly allergic reactions when you eat preserved foods. In 1989 specialists did extensive research on packaged, canned, bagged foods, and all preserved beverages. They found out that they cause the majority of the diseases you suffer from because your bloodstream reacts to the chemicals they use to preserve them. You also did a study yourself to gather information to show consumers that they have to be careful and eat more fresh food. Certainly, we should eat home-cooked meals. You have tried to tell your children, wife, relatives, close friends, and even me not to eat junk food every time they need something to fill an empty stomach. You have tried to teach your three boys to eat fresh and healthy food, but they didn't want to listen to you. When they needed to fill their belly with greasy junk food, they ignored your recommendations."

Food Allergies

"Now I am going to say something very important about these food allergies that have messed up your health. As I said before, you were eight years of age when your first major stroke demolished your body; for several months, you were completely paralyzed. Your face twisted back, your legs bent to your stomach. Your parents took you to the hospital. They ran all the tests for a stroke and for a heart attack, but everything was negative. Doctors couldn't give an accurate diagnostic report or prescribe medicines to cure you.

"You spent a long time in the hospital. The doctor discharged you two months later so you could die in the comfort of your home. Then one night, you were pronounced dead by the town medic. Twenty minutes later, your breathing came back, and miraculously, healing began. It was a nightmare for you. The pain in your chest was severe, and the people who saw you crawling laughed at you and called you nasty names, such as the Hunchback Charcoal Snail. Bad people picked that awful name because dirt covered your skin and your body was twisted and bent. Your parents couldn't clean you up because the skin on your chest and your back was burned and peeled off. You couldn't take a bath for more than five months. You decided not to go out and stayed for almost two years behind closed doors.

"It is very important to say that you had the drive to spend most of your time exercising and meditating. A female doctor had told you at the hospital that you had a small chance for a full recovery if you did physical therapy, and ate healthily, but you needed to take it easy, rest, and pray a lot.

"Of course, you had that in mind, so you pushed yourself to the limit. It took a while for you to see the improvement. Several months went by, and you were ready to give up. But one day, you turned your neck to the right, you heard a crack, and your head twisted a bit into place. From that moment, you never stopped working out, for you knew that was your only way to recover fully. As a result of the exercise, you got a very athletic and muscular body." I stopped for a second, and jokingly said, "That's the reason why now you date all the pretty girls.

Revelori chuckled. I added, "I give you a high five, and I salute you for your achievement." I added laughing, "And I can only go out with women who are old and fat like me. I guess I deserve them old, fat, wrinkled, and toothless." I looked at him and jabbed his six-pack.

I said, "And this was the first huge challenge you faced as a boy. I have to tell you, it made a big impact on you. Indeed, it changed you; it made you a unique boy. You were, and you are still very spiritual. You knew you were still alive by the grace of God, and Jesus had a special task for you. You didn't have a single doubt in your mind that you were going to be facing tough challenges throughout your life, but Jesus gave you the gift of prayer."

It was around five in the afternoon when I stopped talking. I turned around and walked away. I had taken about twenty paces when I heard Revolori calling me out. "Are you coming tomorrow? If you come, please prepare a better story to tell me."

I replied, "I'll give you a hint. I'll talk about the second stroke you had when you were around twenty-four."

Second Stroke

The next day, I came to the park at around one in the afternoon. I parked on the street, for there was not a single stall available at the park's parking lot.

Revolori was already looking around to spot me. In a couple of minutes, I was standing next to him. We walked to a metal bench and sat. Revolori was relaxed, and I said in a soft voice, "I'm already here." He looked at me. By now, he knew that I had been talking about him and his own personal story with many true events about his life from the very beginning. He was aware that I was going to speak about his second stroke. He wanted to ask me how I knew about his personal life history, but he didn't dare to ask me.

Revolori cut a branch from a bush next to him, and he asked me, "Are you ready to start, or is there something wrong? I'm ready to hear my second stroke narrated by you. But be honest please." Revolori pleaded with me.

"I will, and I solemnly promise," I replied.

Of course, I went on to talk about Revolori's second stroke to my only listener, who was heeding the tale of his own biography. I spoke with the elegance that a professional gardener could inject to the first ten words that came out of my toothless mouth.

"You were twenty-two years old, and you were going to California State University Fullerton. You were majoring in writing. Am I right?" I asked. He nodded. "And you were taking a heavy load of classes. In that semester, you were taking sixteen units and you had a full- time job. Certainly, you were abusing your body, both physically and mentally.

"It was December 31, 1986, on the last day of the year." I took a breath, and said with a tiny but noticeable headshake, "It was very cold. You were working swing shift alone. You worked as a security guard that night. You kept patrolling the premises of a construction site. You were guarding a fancy home's construction track. It was dark, and you carried a mall flashlight in your hand. You sat in the passenger seat in your small car, a Ford Mercury Topaz. It was around 10:15 at night. You had been sitting down for about twenty-five minutes observing and reporting. It was time to make your once-an-hour round. You stretched your legs to get up; they didn't respond, you got afraid and rolled your body to the ground. You landed on dirt, nails, splinters, mud, logs, and all kinds of other sharp tools and equipment. Luckily, you didn't get any bruises or cuts when you fell. You dragged yourself about a hundred yards to the gate; it took you a good twenty-three minutes to make it. The gate had a gap in the middle; it was big enough for you to go through it. You fit in the hole, and you crawled and moved forward. You had turned into a wounded snake shedding its skin."

I took a long break; at this point, I gave Revolori a napkin to wipe away tears that were trickling from his eyes. A few seconds later, he told me loud and clear, "Please go on with the story." He said that he was not crying, that the tears were permanent allergy reactions he got from the strokes. This was his last sentence: "Every time I speak or listen for a long time to sad stories, my eyes get watery."

I continued telling him, "That night you spent twenty minutes on the side of the highway, hoping someone spotted you and called 911. In a matter of minutes, you heard an ambulance wailing in the distance. The Irvine paramedics picked you up and took you to a nearby hospital in Tustin. You were admitted and spent a week in intensive care. You were discharged eight days later with a bunch of medicine and prescriptions.

"For the second time, you started the hard work of physical therapy, speech therapy, and you got psychological help and instructions to take your medicine in time. You missed your current classes for the entire semester, but two semesters later you went back to California State

University Fullerton using a walker. Two years later, you were fully recovered and working as normally as you did before the stroke. It was a terrible time for you, because you didn't have a single family member or relative to take care of you. You were in a wheelchair while you were learning to walk. But willpower and strength in prayer made you a winner again."

Revolori cut me off and said, "I have learned that if we trust in God and do the hard work, everything is possible, and we all can achieve our goals. Back then I set my mind on healing, and I intend to testify it to future generations. Especially, I will encourage young children who don't know how to take care of their bodies and spirit, to take it easy and pray."

Walt Disney Pictures

"I also know about your third stroke," I told Revolori, "and I'm going to talk about it now. I am sure you're wondering how I got to learn so much about your personal life. Maybe God told me to tell you, to prepare you for future events that are going to harm you."

It was Friday at noon, a sunny hot day that I visited Revolori at the park. I had a Coca-Cola can in my hand. I raised it to take a huge sip, Revolori was, as usual, drinking water, and eating a salmon salad, and fruit for lunch. I was chewing non-stop on my French fries, and eating my fat, greasy cheeseburger.

Two Jehovah's Witness men were walking around the park trying to fish out on dry land. They had their eyes set on Revolori; they thought he was an easy catch. They approached us. One came to Revolori, and the other chose to talk to me. They lectured us on their religion without a good result, and they gave up soon. They had not realized that Revolori wasn't an easy target.

Revolori shook his head and said, "They are bad sellers. Certainly, they should get more training from a professional business coach."

I stood up and cleared my throat and started. "Now I need to go on with the third stroke that hit you not long ago, and we are wasting time. I'm sure you are ready to listen." I continued to speak about Revolori's third miraculous healing. "It was 3:33 in the afternoon, July 31, 2008, on a hot sunny afternoon in Burbank. Theresa Dahlquist, your son's talent agent and you had a meeting with the Disney Music Group on the seventeenth floor. When the meeting was over, you felt a nerve pull, and your brain couldn't control your body. You were getting weak on the right side. You did not want to tell the agent about it, but you knew that you were almost fainting. Somehow you managed to drive back home. The drive was about ten minutes, the traffic was light, and you made it in a short period of time to Vineland and Ventura Boulevard in Studio City. You got into your apartment, and your two boys and wife waved at you. You didn't say a word, and you just went straight to the bedroom and got into bed. It was 4:55 when you fell asleep. Your wife went to sleep at 11:00 and by that time you were already paralyzed and blind, but she did not notice it. You wanted so badly to tell her that you were dying, but you couldn't because you had lost your voice too.

"The next morning at 05:45, your wife got up for a trip to the bathroom. When she came back to bed, she saw you and started to scream. She called out to your two sons to get up. They put you in her car in a matter of minutes and took you to Dr. Richard Han, your family doctor. At Dr. Han's office, two nurses rushed you to the exam room. After a quick exam, Dr. Han sent you immediately to Western Memorial Hospital in Anaheim. At once, you were admitted, and they took care of your blood pleasure because it was very high. The tests were ordered to make sure your brain and heart were working properly. Doctor Han ran diagnostic tests for stroke, but all the tests came back negative, so they couldn't give you the right diagnosis nor give you medicine to ease your suffering. You were admitted for three days, and on the fourth day Dr. Han discharged you. By the way, on the second day you spent in the hospital, you learned that your twelve-year-old son started to smoke and sell pot. Your wife was letting your brother Henry's son, Josh, supply your son with marijuana. You were surprised to find out that your wife and brother let him become a drug user and abuser, and the worse thing was that they were hooking your son to profit from drugs.

"On that second night, your older son Mario Jr. came to the hospital and stayed overnight, and he told you about the whole drug deal. He wept on your shoulder, and he begged you and said, 'Please don't die, Pops. We need you so bad, bro, don't leave us yet.' You made a promise to him that you were going to ask God in your payers to heal you, and you would do anything required in your human strength to make it alive. And you would live to continue to take care of them. When you got back home, you had already made your mind up that you were not going to give up. From that day forward, you took very good care of yourself, doing your exercises as the physical therapist had shown you to do them. You practiced your speech exercises on time, and as often as you could. Your wife made sure to cook healthy food and served it to you at the right time. Tony, your younger son, never left your bed. He was taking good care of you after school, on the weekends, and holidays. And from that moment, you started to call him Dr. Tony.

"You prayed several times a day all the time. You were convinced that your spirit needed to be in an awesome relationship with God. As a Christian, you knew Jesus was going to heal you with his divine power. There was not a single doubt that he was with you 24/7. One night at three in the morning, you were praying, and Jesus was in front of you. You saw him with the eyes of your physical body standing by your bed; he spoke to you with authority. You heard him clearly, his words sounded so powerful and convincing. He was gently putting his prophesy into your brain.

"He revealed to you, 'On Wednesday at three in the afternoon, you are going to heal completely.' You were awakened. It wasn't a dream, and for a moment you thought that you were going crazy. At that second, you believed it was just your imagination, and that the devil was playing a trick on you. A voice whistled to your ears telling you not to trust in God. Immediately you rebuked Satan in the name of Jesus, you had faith in the words of the Lord, and you believed in the message that he had given you. It was a Saturday morning when Jesus spoke to you. You decided to tell it to two people. You chose your mother and your wife. You thought they could be your witnesses if the prophecy came true. They both laughed at you when you told them that Jesus came to you and that he had let you see him. Convincingly, you told them Jesus talked to you, and he told you that he was going to cure you on a Wednesday at three in the afternoon. Your wife told your mother that she feared for you. She thought you were losing your mind. Your dear mom had the same words to share with your dad who was the only one who supported and believed you. He was sure the revelation was going to come true. Truly, he was certain that Jesus was going to heal you at the appointed time.

"It was a long time of waiting for you, and for Wednesday to come. The words were spinning in your mind, and they were driving you crazy. There was no room to think about other things in your brain. You were expecting the miracle to come true and to heal you. You kept guessing how it was going to be done. Jesus's words were echoing in your head; your brain repeated these words every five to ten minutes: 'The Lord had told me, the Lord had told me, the Lord had told me...' And your eyes never stopped seeing the image of his face and his body standing in front of you.

"Sure enough, Wednesday morning came. You were sad and worried. 'This is it,' you told to yourself. Everybody was getting ready to leave, the adults were going to work, and your sons were heading to school. You wanted to hug and talk to them, but you couldn't move out of bed or talk to tell them how much you loved them. At seven forty-five, everybody had left but your wife. She brought a glass of water and a small cup of chicken soup to your bed. You got your voice back for a few seconds and reminded her about Jesus's promise to you. For some reason, you asked her to go buy honey and to give you a spoonful. She answered, 'Luckily, six months ago your sister Patty sent you a bottle of medicinal honey from the Mayan Mountains of Guatemala, and I saved it for you. I'll go get it right now.'

It was 8:03 in the morning. She gave you two small half spoons, for you couldn't swallow anything without choking. Even so, you almost choked to death when the liquid went down your throat. She had to help you to keep your head up. The reaction was immediate. You felt that the honey traveled to the center top of your head right on top of the soft spot.

At three in the afternoon the same day, it began to press down from the top of your head. Thick saliva, phlegm, and blood came out of your eyes, ears, mouth, nose, and all the liquids that were coming out almost choked you to death again. The healing was happening as Jesus had announced it.

"You had to keep your head hanging down for three weeks to let your brain drain all the dirt and the blood clot that the stroke had left in your head. Seven days after you drank the honey, a piece of bone came out from your left eye. The bone was the size and the shape of a tooth. It started moving from the left side of your head, and it went to your temple, then it moved to your eyebrow and out it came from the corner of your left eye. It took seven days to come out. You kept counting the days."

At this point Revolori interrupted me. He chose to finish it up. "After the first piece came out, I felt a little better. The honey was working so well and pushed out of my head a total of seven pieces. That was the beginning of the miracle Jesus had promised me, and in three years I got a full recovery. My third big stroke went to the past. I went back to work as I did before, and I was telling my testimony to friends and relatives how Jesus told me ahead of time that he was going to heal me at a fixed day, and it happened at the time he promised me."

Revolori stopped talking, and I looked around for a few seconds, and then I got up to stretch myself. Revolori turned to me and placed his hand on my belly and told me, "Dear Knus, you've got to lose weight, you're so fat. A stroke can hit you like a hurricane." He chuckled, and then he said, "I'm joking, buddy, you're just fine the way you are."

I was sad and with broken words, I warned him. "Now you know, I have been narrating your biography. I won't tell you how I got all the information. But I must warn you ahead of time you'll suffer a fourth stroke. You'll lose your health, your assets, and all your family members, relatives, and close friends. When the time comes, you are going to put it in writing yourself to continue your life story. You won't need me anymore."

The Arts

Knus predicted my stroke caused by poisoning and the miraculous healing that would follow. I thought he had made up all the predictions that he told me three weeks after my wife separated from me on February 28, 2011. Almost five months later, my sons didn't want to see or talk to me anymore. On March 10, 2014, I got married to Margarita.

Knus last talked to me in the fourth week of March 2011, and he told me what was going to happen to my family and me. He and I were sitting in my car listening to the car radio. I put my feet on the dashboard to rest my legs.

This time, he was the listener, and I led the conversation. Knus listened to what I had to say, and I let out my first word telling him about my present life. I shared with him my faith in Jesus. "Today, it is my turn," I started, "I'll tell you my biggest accomplishment so far. What I'm going to talk about—it's art, music, writing, tricks, hacking, poisoning, killing, and finally my fourth stroke." Of course, I was playing around with him. "It going to take me a long time—I mean, many days, months, and years to finish it. I'll jot it down, but your prophecy will never happen. But I promise you'll be the first person to know if it becomes a reality.

"Meanwhile, I'm going to be honest with you," I said. "I have a close-to-perfect relationship with my wife. I have three talented sons, a heck of a great family. Our separation is temporary, and in a couple of months, we'll be back together. My boys are artists, I'm their manager, and soon we'll start an arts academy. I will coach acting, my older son will teach music—guitar, bass, piano, voice, and drums—and my younger son will give painting lessons. And my gorgeous wife will have enough time and money to shop all the time." Knus just shook his head and he said good-bye forever. I never saw him again.

Music

One evening in South Central Los Angeles, May 2014, Anna begged me to teach her everything I knew about music, including singing, songwriting, piano, guitar, bass, and drums. She talked to me for almost an hour to convince me. Finally, I said yes, on one condition. "What's that condition, Dad?" she replied.

Cautiously, I said, "You have to get the approval from your mom first. She instantly became sad because she knew Margarita wasn't going to let her waste time practicing music." Anna begged me to go ask Margarita myself. After a long dad and daughter debate, I agreed to speak to Margarita on her behalf.

I spent a few sleepless nights finding a way to make Margarita say yes. I was about to give up, but Anna meant the world to me, and she was everything I had. I was not going to surrender that easy. So, I decided to give it a try. After two weeks of intense talking and bribing Margarita, she said yes. But the whole thing cost me a couple of thousand dollars, a trip to Vegas, a few expensive dinners at fancy restaurants, and some jewels. But every penny I spent was worth it.

Eventually, we went to Guitar Center. Anna purchased a bass guitar, an acoustic guitar, and a digital keyboard. I taught her how to play them, and she also took songwriting and singing lessons. She was blessed because I have a minor in music, and I was her private music coach. In three months, she was already writing, arranging, and singing her original songs. On November 2014, at the age of nine, she recorded her first original single called "I Say." She uploaded it to YouTube, and a seven-year-old girl listened to it and loved it. The little girl's name was Heligar Greenbells. She sent an email to Anna to congratulate her, and she became her first die-hard fan. One year later, Heligar was diagnosed with terminal cancer. Her doctor told her mother she had three days to live. Anna sent her the link to listen to her song "Hold Me Closer" that she had just released. Heligar's mom replied and told Anna that Heligar was going to die in three days. She said that Heligar had listened over and over to Anna's first song "I Say," and she wanted to leave this world listening to it. As soon as Anna got Heligar's mother's email, she burst into tears. I went over and hugged her, but I couldn't hold back my tears either, and as I was reading the email, I joined her and wept. I fell on my knees, and so did Anna. We prayed for Heligar's healing for about an hour. Margarita came to pray with us. I kept praying and crying the whole afternoon.

The next day, an email was sent to my inbox. Anna read it, and this time she was crying with happiness. She called me to go to the computer screen. Heligar's mom said, "Change of plans. The doctor just called me and told me that the impossible has happened. He doesn't believe it, and he doesn't have any idea how it came to pass. Mysteriously, Heligar has been fully cured." I knew that Jesus had healed her. I felt the force of the Holy Spirit had poured onto the little girl when we were praying the day before. Anna wasn't surprised, for she was used to praying five to ten times a day with me. She had seen Jesus's healings herself, and she trusted, and believed in him.

Anna released "Hold Me Closer" and "My Babe" in May 2016. A Hollywood Records owner and producer heard the songs and contacted me; he offered me a three-year recording agreement. The deal didn't go through because she was a minor. Heligar moved from New Jersey to a small countryside town in England, where they are originally from. Anna and Heligar still write to each other.

Acting

Two weeks after the music deal failed, Anna pleaded with me to help her with acting. I agreed and we started a new venture because we lived in the heart of Hollywood, and I had done some acting myself. First, I paid Cynthia Bain Acting Kids, a professional private acting coach, to teach her the fundamentals of acting and to introduce her to the entertainment industry. Anna signed up with Polygon, a boutique talent agency in Burbank, in June 2016, and the owner of the agency chose a different acting school for her.

Long before, Knus had warned me about the fourth stroke, but I thought he was wrong, and it wasn't going to come true. Sadly, it was true. I thought he was joking when he told me that I was going to be talking and writing about a Dart Frog poisoning that would mimic a fourth stroke. But I was mistaken about his prediction.

Anna wasn't learning anything, but her agent wanted me to keep her in the school that the Polygon Talent Agency owner had referred me to. I found a solution to the problem after a couple of weeks of thinking. I cancelled the classes and started coaching her myself. When the agent asked about the coaching lessons, I answered that she was doing a great job in his friend's acting institution.

I had the experience and the contacts, for I had coached actors Tony Revolori, Mario Revolori Jr., and many others for fifteen years. It took me a month to get her ready for auditions. A few weeks went by, and two casting directors auditioned her for adult roles, knowing that she was only eleven years of age. Both casting directors were impressed and told the producers and directors of the projects that they had never seen an actress as brilliant as Anna in the entire time they had worked in the entertainment industry. She learned quickly to write movie scripts. She began to work on two feature films at the same time. She got to page 35 on her screenplay called "Out Crying." She told me about the plot, and it seemed she enjoyed the whole thing, but suddenly, she stopped writing it. I didn't bother to ask her why she had quit.

MegAm

Screenplay

I started to work on a superhero movie entitled "MegAm" several weeks after Anna began her screenplay. We made a bet. I promised her I'd give her three hundred dollars, and I'd buy her the latest editing programs—Final Cut and Pro Tools—if she finished her script first. I wasn't going to give her chances; she knew I wasn't that type of dad. If she wanted to win, we needed to do it fair and square. She went back to write her screenplay "Out Crying" to win and to get the cash.

Anna had begun to write her project a few months before me. The idea about MegAm's story came so fast to my mind. Usually, I come up with project titles and with great topics quickly and easily. For me to write any type of story is a pleasure and therapy, because I love creative writing. Many times, I have written songs in twenty to forty minutes. MegAm is short for Mega American Superhero. It was unique, and all the sketches for the characters were landing on my mind like magnets. Minutes later, the plot was sinking into my brain. I had to make a quick choice to write the screenplay or draw the characters first. Anna was looking at me; she knew that I had something big and cool in my thoughts. I shared them with her, and I asked her which one to start first. I shouldn't have told her that, because she was a child, and children love to draw and color. So, she said to begin drawing the characters.

Soon, Anna handed me a pencil, some crayons, and a few sheets of printing paper. I wasn't expecting that, but my brain had stored all the characters, and it was ready to let them out and stamp them on the white sheet of paper. I didn't have any idea that "MegAm" was going to be the project that triggered my forced stroke. Immediately, I shared with my daughter the following characters: MegAm, MerAm, Lucy Fir Van Ahn, Ben Crook, Don Weiss, and Fir Barc (the Crab).

Storyline

"MegAm" is a cool and touching comic book, and a superhero feature film script. It tells the story of a global criminal organization that gets together to execute all the children of the world under eighteen years of age in a single day. The group of criminals led by their leader, Lucy Fir Van Ahn, want to find a super powerful wonder potion so they can have eternal life. They have a team of scientists working around the clock in a clandestine laboratory in Silicon Valley. Lucy Fir's plans are to kill all the children of the world and force same-sex marriage only in order to stop reproduction of new human beings. Since they are going to live forever, they don't want to overpopulate the planet. Everything is under control, even the magic medicine has been developed, but Lucy Fir is not aware that MegAm, the great American superhero, is on a mission from God to stop them. MegAm organizes his own defense plans. He chooses MerAm and the billionaire Don Weiss to fight back. Lucy Fir and her people will pick the time to gather all the children in a secluded private beach in Southern California. She'll schedule the slaughter as soon as she gets her hands on the eternal life drug. MegAm's top priority is to stop the production of the magic pills, and to steal the formula and stop all production of more medicine.

Characters

MEGAM: Mike Watters, a tall, skinny young boy, walks along a dirt road in the countryside. He strolls toward a tall tree standing majestically on top of a hill. Suddenly, three men from a strange world block his path and stop him. The three strangers tell him that he had been chosen to save all the children of the world. They tell him that it'll take place during a one-year period, and they'll return to meet him again and give him superpowers. Fourteen months later, Mike Watters is driving on the highway near the town of Salem, Virginia, and the three men show up again and vest him in a fancy and awesome superpower suit, naming him MegAm. This is how the superhero comes to fight and to save the planet.

The creation of this character was also going to put me in intensive care for seventeen days at a private hospital within a few months. Anna kept on writing on her own screenplay, and the challenge was giving me strength and I was having a lot of fun. I hadn't started to write MegAm, yet. I was working hard on the drawings, but both Anna and I were pleased with the characters. At this point, even Margarita was supporting me.

MegAm was sketched on paper in three days; it was kind of cute, and a unique character. Neither Anna nor I ever expected that it was going to be that good.

I was ready to color it when Anna grabbed it without asking and chose the colors. She was done coloring in a hurry. Margarita and I approved it. She chose a yellow color for the suit, and blue-brownish diamond eyes. We added a computer attached to his chest, a radar antenna, and a silver magnetic shield in the back. The front clipped to his belt to stop and redirect any kind of weapon launch at it, and to send back nuclear missile heads to its attackers.

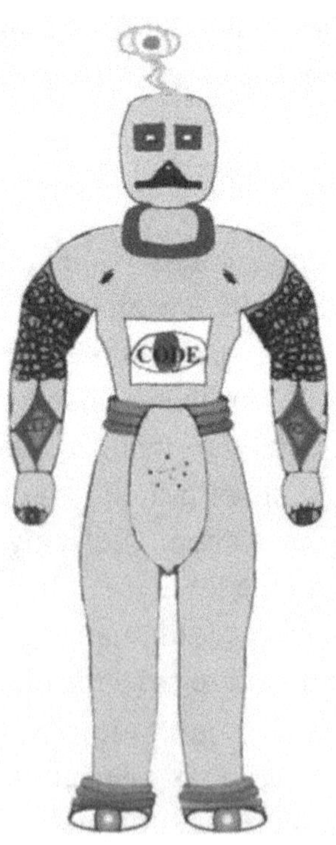

BEN CROOK: I started to shape my second character, Ben Crook, but it didn't work at all. Margarita was watching me and saw me having a hard time getting the right sketch. She approached me and offered suggestions, and helped me draw it. I had to admit she was a better cartoonist and painter than I was. She finished it in two days. But it wasn't even close to what I had in mind. She drew a cartoon character with short, handicapped arms; it was a cliché, no originality.

Margarita didn't want to give up her work. She argued that because the name of the character was Crook, the actual picture must be crooked in shape. Anna gave me a quick look of disapproval. I winked and she understood. We needed to let Margarita make the choice. I thought it was time to move on, and we began to work on the next character. Anna chose Lucy Fir Van Ahn.

LUCY FIR VAN AHN: Anna and Margarita started to argue about choosing to draw Lucy Fir. Eventually, Margarita got to work on the character. In a short period of time, she showed me the final piece of art. She was completely sure that we were going to agree with her, but she was way off with the details I had given her.

She took it literally from the title once again, and drew a character with horns and witch's fingernails.

Anna uploaded the three characters to YouTube without telling me. It was a big mistake that we couldn't correct, and months later, this error would send me to the hospital. In a matter of minutes, casting director Stuart Stone apparently saw them and contacted me, offering his help. The next day, I read the email and found out that he had seen my project.

Instantly, I ordered Anna to take the characters off. She deleted them right away, but it was a little too late. A couple of minutes after we got the characters off, I received another email from the casting director, promising Anna that he wasn't going to steal the work. He told me that he wasn't only a casting director in Hollywood, but a top producer as well, and he loved my project.

Two weeks later, he and I were hacked by a professional assassin. Certainly, I was going to be fooled by a professional hacker. Meanwhile, Stuart Stone gave Anna free top-of-the-line printing software to work on MegAm's comic book. A day later, he suggested that I make changes to Ben Crook and Lucy Fir Van Ahn. Anna was already sketching MerAm, the second main character.

MERAM is a fourteen- to sixteen-year-old girl. She is MegAm's half-sister, but she doesn't know it. She's the only person in the world who knows MegAm's true identity, and where his superpowers come from, and she sees him without the suit on. MerAm is a supermodel girl with long hair, and she's very attractive.

She's MegAm assistant. She passes the messages to Don Weiss because MegAm talks in code. He's invisible, and he can't show himself to the public. They see him only when he's on a mission, fighting, or rescuing somebody.

DON WEISS: He's a billionaire businessman with a big heart. He loves to play golf and to make big business deals. He's good with children. The men in yellow informed MegAm that he could trust Mr. Weiss. They gave him the list of the people he needed to contact for the rescuing mission to stop the evil plan of Lucy Fir Van Ahn. Don Weiss wears thick red and blue ties and business suits all the time, even when he's playing golf.

FIR BARC: The Fir Barc is the most powerful piece of warfare machine that Lucy Fir Van Ahn has built. It's a huge submarine crab apparatus loaded with nuclear weapons. It runs on rails in six tunnels dug under the sea to connect all continents in the world. It can also swim and can jump a mile high.

The headquarters are built on a secret private beach near Los Angeles, California, with connections to small stations near the Hamburg area in Germany, in China, a small station in South America, in Australia, and South Africa.

The Crab is where Lucy Fir's office and secret place is located. Personally, she plans the attacks from there. She also approves and supervises all deals and meetings from the crab. Fir Barc has been engineered to demolish one quarter of the earth's surface in one day. It's loaded with six powerful nuclear missiles aimed at all the continents and ready to launch. They're labeled so they can be launched and fired at all six continents at the same time.

Character Changes

Two weeks had passed since I started MegAm. Anna and I had been working very hard, and all the characters were ready. I wasn't happy with Lucy Fir Van Ahn or Ben Crook, but we welcomed them in the meantime. In the back of my mind, I wanted to change Lucy Fir and Ben Crook. I had the idea to draw them again and sketch them my way. However, it was a huge problem. I had to fight Margarita first, and I knew she wasn't going to talk to me for a week if I changed them. After much thinking, I gave up and started the writing of the screenplay.

The plot was clicking in my head, and like a sponge, my brain was squeezing the words out, the sentences, the paragraphs were easy to write. Then the pages were increasing, and Anna and I were very pleased with the whole project.

In a few days, I had written thirty-three pages, and I was enjoying the writing. We were working on the comic book at the same time. I knew God was watching out for me, but Satan was working through the fake casting agent. I stopped for a second to catch my breath, and then I said to myself with a sad look in my eyes, "A stroke." Water ran down my left eye, like a cascade gushing from a cliff. I thought and I feared for the first time that a fourth stroke could be around the corner, ready to hit me. I took a long pause again. I reached for my green, plastic cup half-full of water. Knus, who was my friend and my landscaping worker for many years, was close to being right in his prophecy. He was an interesting fellow with a lot of wisdom and a bunch of other things to show and teach me. So, I was remembering that Knus had warned me of a fourth deadly stroke.

It took me a long time to drink my water. I enjoyed it so much, and every drop of water that went down my throat gave energy to my spirit and body. I kept silent for a good five minutes. I was intrigued at that moment. I wished Knus was near me to tell me the rest of the story. I pretended that I was patient, but my ears were sharp to go back to the listening. I had already finished my water, and he was drinking his second Coca-Cola bottle. To kill time, he kept his fingers busy rubbing the glass.

I came back to the present and stood up and did some stretching exercises with my hands, legs, and body. I was about to sit, but first I started to do some vocals for my speech exercises and to relax my nerves. I was remembering everything Knus told me on the last visit he paid me at the park. Where was my dear mentor, Knus, to ask him questions? I wanted to turn back time and to press him to tell me who wanted to kill me, who was paying for my assassination, and who had been the whistle-blower about my past life. But I couldn't. I just hoped and prayed that that fatal stroke Knus had talked about was only his imagination.

Real Casting Agency and Fake Casting Agency

Knus's face was still in my mind; I couldn't jump into the present. I remembered one time that he was sad. He took a big breath, cracked, and pulled his fingers to relax. He said, "Now just listen, Revolori." He roared with a medium tone of his hoarse and powerful voice. "There are some legal issues, and I can't give you the true name of the whistle- blower." He asked me, "What do you suggest, Mr. Revolori?" He stared at me for a long time, and then he marched away giving me a military salute.

After a long silence and thinking to bring my mind to present time, I came up with a fast solution. My feelings guided me to forget about Knus and not to think about the stroke prediction. Here's how my contact with Stuart Stone from Stuart Stone Casting began.

In May 2016, the real talent agent sent me a casting notification telling me that Anna had an audition for a female pop star project called Kid Union. She needed to prepare two songs either original or cover. Anna sent the self-tape audition, and was immediately picked among the first three finalists.

Stuart Stone told me, "Anna is going to get picked because her talent is over the top. There is no other singer who matches her voice, her dancing, and performance style from thousands of auditions I have received from around the world."

Two weeks passed and the casting director had been sending me emails every other day to keep me posted about the status of the casting process. Suddenly, he stopped sending me notifications for a week. Anna and I started to get nervous. We just kept waiting, hoping, and praying.

One morning, I opened the inbox to read my most recent emails. I saw the email, and the casting director said, "Mr. Revolori, I've got good and not-so-good news." And I read it over quickly because Anna was around kind of taking a look over my shoulder. I didn't want her to read it because I had a strange feeling that something wasn't right.

The email started: "Hello, Mr. Revolori, I have two pieces of news for you. One is extremely good and the other one not so good." I continued reading the next sentence, and he wrote this: "I'll write about the less important first."

This was his message: "I advise you not to tell Anna now, prepare her first because she's a teenager, and this will give her a sad emotion. She wasn't chosen for this gig. I don't know what in tarnation…those stupid directors and producers are so ignorant and chose a crappy singer. They had told me that they were looking for the best of the best singers, dancers, and performers, and she had to be beautiful and attractive. I am not a racist, don't get me wrong, but they chose the worst of the worst artists, and the least attractive. The producers and directors cast an Indian girl—I mean, a Native American singer. Your daughter has a million angels in her heart singing with her, and I mean it, not a joke."

I paused then I continued reading the next paragraph. Stuart Stone wrote, "This is the good news: the producers wanted to steal your song, but they found out that you copyrighted it already. They got furious and that's the reason why they didn't book Anna." Of course, this was one of the authentic emails sent to me by the real casing director.

Two months later a fake casting agent from Frankfurt, Germany, started to hack my computer and to break into the real casting director computer to access communication and data on the system.

A flashback about what Knus had told me came to my mind. He had been telling me amazing stories from the first time he came to my house. When I fixed my eyes straight into his for the last time, I was terrified that I was not going to see him again. I should have asked him if he was narrating my life story on purpose. Why, he had even used my last name from the very start. It was not possible that he knew every little secret that hid in the deepest part of my heart by chance.

By now, I had guessed that God himself had told him the story of my life. I should have questioned and compelled him to tell me who was behind the whole thing. In fact, I should have demanded he give me the names of those who would plot against me. I should have advised him to get a lawyer and to be prepared to hear from mine. Maybe he would have gotten nervous and passed out, or he would keep his cool. I couldn't be sure if that was a spiritual revelation given to me about my future life.

The last sentence Knus told me rang in my ears. Clearly he said, "Mr. Revolori, it's been a great pleasure to tell you a part of your amazing and unique life story." He nodded and paused before continuing. "It's a shame that you won't see me anymore. I'm afraid that I won't be able to finish telling you about your deadly last stroke. I urge you please to continue writing it yourself. I hope I'll see you again in the distant blue sky."

I interrupted him. "But you'll come tomorrow, right?"

He replied, "You won't need me anymore, kid. You'll know the end of the story of your life soon, and you have to write it yourself. The rest of the tale of your life is still blowing in the wind. I warn you it's going to be a rough and tough journey for you. Life will be painful for you and your family. You'll lose everything, including your health and family. In the end, you'll make it, and your spirit won't be touched. I'll pray for you, my friend.

"I tell you, if you stop praying, you won't make it. Be strong, kid, and trust the Lord with all your heart. Certainly, your life's a mystery full of wonderful events. Just imagine, you could be the first man to ever survive four major strokes and come back to life after death two times in forty years. As I already said, your life is a myth."

Real Casting Agency Last Contacts

These were the last calls and emails I received from the real Stuart Stone Casting. Stuart Stone was in love with Anna's singing and writing style. He loved her performances and dancing movements. He let me know that he was going to do everything in his power to refer her to his friends in the music industry.

Stuart Stone also told me that he knew some top-of-the-line hit producers in Hollywood and around the world. He promised me that he was going to make personal referrals to recommend Anna. He advised me to cut two radio-ready songs at the legendary Pacifique Recording Studios in North Hollywood. He even contacted Simon Cowell from "America's Got Talent" and scheduled Anna an audition for the 2017 season.

Anna and I wrote, arranged, and produced the two songs. Grammy winner Ted Greenberg and Grammy nominee Tony Valenziano engineered the songs. I got the radio-ready EP in my hands. I contacted the casting director Stuart Stone on behalf of Anna to discuss her material. I notified him that the songs were ready for release and for submissions to labels, A&Rs, and managers.

Stuart Stone received the MP3 files for the songs "Cool Off" and "Count Me On." He was very impressed with her vocal abilities and gave me the go-ahead to submit the songs to big labels only. The casting agent's older son heard the songs, and he loved Anna's voice. He told his dad that she had the voice of an angel inside her heart, and that he wanted to meet her in person one day. Stuart Stone's two daughters heard the songs too and immediately fell in love with them. He asked them to pick the best song and they chose "Cool Off.". I mailed them to A&Rs and to several music labels and agencies. Stuart Stone even provided me with the contact names, numbers, and addresses for the top five major music labels in Hollywood: Disney Music Media Group, Atlantic Records, Warner Bros, Sony Music, and Hollywood Records.

I emailed a bunch of CDs to labels, radio stations, A&Rs, online programs, and licensing companies. Massive CDs and emails were sent that week all over the United States and Europe.

Record Deal

In May 2016, the president of Hollywood Records had listened to Anna's single, "Hold Me Closer." Producer and co-owner, Robert Dawson, sent me an email telling me to prepare Anna for a live audition. The two producers and owners of the record company were very taken with her signing and worked hard to sign a record deal with her.

The first email from Robert Dawson said, "I am the co-owner and producer of Hollywood Records. We'll review the EP submission for Anna Revolori." He wrote, "You'll be waiting for an email either from me, or the co-owner, Shelton Shannon."

Mrs. Shannon sent a special message, "Anna is very talented. She has a unique niche, a deep voice with high and low range, and is very attractive. I'll give you a good advice from the very deepest part of my heart. Never ever let this girl go, never. Don't even think about quitting the race, always support her as your client. We also know that she's your daughter through IMDB. Please, I ask you not to let this beautiful, extraordinary voice die. Take good care of her and always. No matter what happens, take her to coaches and learn, so you yourself can teach her. We are one of the few labels that let you manage your own children, so if the chairman, Mr. Howard Hollywood, decides to hire her, I myself will ask him to let you be her manager. I have been a long time in this beautiful business, and I tried to quit with my son, but I learned that we have to be with our children always, no matter the faces that they are making behind our back. Now that my son is dead, he said in the last moments of his short life, 'Mom, you are the best person that I have ever met.' I am really proud of that. We never find anybody like her. We would be delighted to work together."

It was a lifetime dream to sign a record deal for Anna, and I kept counting every single day for the entire month. The waiting was long and painful.

Four weeks passed, and we were getting impatient and losing hope. I thought they were not going to contact me anymore. Anna came to me one morning, and crying, she softly mumbled the words, "Daddy, I've already given up. I'm sure they're not going to call me anymore. All my dreams of becoming a pop star were just dreams and will always be just dreams. They'll never come true."

I tried to cheer her up as best as I could and, holding my breath with a cracking voice, I told her, "Sweetie, you have to be patient. We must wait a little longer. Let's give them another week, and we might hear something good from them." I hugged her and gave her a big fatherly kiss on her cheek. I got back the sweetest smile ever. I've never seen Anna so happy and patient.

She told me, "It sounds like a good plan, Dad. We'll wait as long as it takes." She thanked me and ran to her bedroom.

The next day Anna woke up early and stormed into my room in tears. She sat down on the edge of my bed, and she leaned to give me a kiss on my forehead. She suggested that I call Hollywood Records. She was shooting me questions like arrows, but I managed to give a satisfactory answer to all of them. Suddenly, I asked her to go get me a glass of water. I took a breath to relax and think of how to answer and not to make her sad. She ran out and a few seconds later, she was back. She still asked me a couple more questions, and I was giving her all the time, help, and support that I was able to provide.

Those daily conversations between Anna and I continued for ten more days. I didn't want to disappoint her or make her sad, but I was certain Hollywood Records was not going to contact me anymore.

Hollywood Records' Last Email

One day, at 11:19 in the morning, the last email from Hollywood Records came to my inbox. I couldn't believe it because I had already given up hope, and I rushed to read it. I kept looking around, for I knew my daughter was nearby, and I didn't want her to know yet. Here is what the email from Shannon Shelton said:

"This is Shannon Shelton from Hollywood Records. I'm here to share the sad news with you. We were not able to process your submission for Anna Revolori. Here are the main reasons why we couldn't go forward:

Our policy for teenagers under 18 is that we can't audition or sign a contract with minors who have not yet appeared on a Disney Channel or in a Disney XD show. Even if it is a minor role, or as a guest star; it's still acceptable.

We just signed a record deal for three years with a brand-new band and are not able to take auditions or sign any new artist for at least six months.

Look, Mr. Revolori, please do not share the news with Anna yet. Tell her very gently. The reason is that she is young and she'll get very emotional. It's not your fault or her fault that she couldn't audition. I tried my best, but there was no way that I could get you an audition. I swear to God, who is watching us from above, that we had everything ready—contracts, tour dates, and everything packed. But we have to go through a lengthy process to audition someone. We take any auditions from anybody; we like to give everybody a chance. I tell you from the depths of my heart that Anna is the most incredible singer and musician that I have ever seen! Never give up. The entertainment business is a tough industry, but it is very nice at the same time.

I'll give you another tip from my experience: Don't submit her material to small labels; go for the major ones. The reason is that the small boutique labels, as we call them, are just going to want to own the rights to your music. That's why I suggest that you try to get her showcases for labels. That'll lose her shyness, if any.

We appreciate your efforts and hope to hear from you in future. I know this young lady will go far and will have big success in any direction that she goes.

Keep up the good work. I'll tell you a little secret: The Chairman couldn't stop listening to Anna's EP. He was really amazed at her voice. He even said that it was an angel singing and was sure he would never hear a voice like that again!"

When I saw the email, I felt like I was swimming in a cloud across the sea. Thousands of ideas came to me, and I didn't know what emotion to show first. I wanted to laugh, to cry, to sing, to yell, and to jump up and down. My first thought was to call Anna before I even read it.

I took a deep breath to calm myself down. I covered my mouth to block the sound because my brain had already given my tongue and lips the command to call Anna and give her the good news. In my mind, ther was nothing but an certainty that she was going to be signed for a three-year contract.

I lowered my voice, but not enough, and Anna still heard me calling her, and came running from her bedroom. She gave me a sweet, happy hug, then paused a bit, and asked me, "Do you have any good news for me, Daddy? You always call me that quietly when you have a big surprise for me." She was looking me straight in the eye. We both sat in the same chair in front of the computer and read the email together.

When we started reading the second sentence, we stopped. "I'm sorry to be the one to give you the bad news." We were very sad, and Anna had tears running down her cheeks. I cheered her up, giving her a big hug and encouraging her, saying that more gigs were going to come soon. I said to her that all we needed to do was keep knocking on more doors. It took me a couple of days of constant reassurance to calm her down.

I was praying every two to three hours, and two days later, Anna came out with a big smile on her face, for she had locked herself in her room after the sad news. She spent days weeping and shaking; one time, she even fainted. I told Margarita that we might need to take her to the doctor, but our prayers and support worked miracles, and she came to her senses sooner than I expected.

We went back to a normal life. Anna kept writing songs, playing her piano and guitar, and started to learn the bass guitar. She got a gig in Los Angeles at the legendary Amplify Theatre. She did a couple of all-ages shows and got great reviews. She also performed at the Chain Reaction Theatre in Anaheim a mile away from Disneyland, the happiest place on Earth.

Email Intercepted

During our search, I received a suspicious email, supposedly from the desk of Stuart Stone. He asked me to change his email address because he had created a new one. Right away, I updated his contact email on my computer and informed him that I already had changed the new one on my computer data system. I was surprised that he answered me immediately; usually it took him three days for a reply.

I wasn't aware that a criminal and professional hacker had intercepted my last email to Stuart Stone. However, I was so happy that he replied quickly that Anna and I read it and sent a reply back. The second email, he answered within minutes. At first, I asked Anna what was on his mind that he was replying to my emails in a hurry. Anna noticed the change and was amazed by how eager he was to answer our emails; we didn't have a clue that something was questionable.

I believed that Stuart Stone was becoming a very close friend of mine, and that he was trying to help Anna because he was very interested in her music. Anna warned me, and she told me, "You have to be careful. Look, Dad, he even wants you to start calling him Stuart instead of Mr. Stone as you've been calling him since I have been auditioning with his agency." She continued giving me her wise counsel: "All I'm saying is, you have to be on the lookout. I know you're a good guy, but others are vultures, and they're willing to sell their souls to the devil for a buck. You gottta think, Dad. Remember how your own sons treat you like a piece of trash. They don't even talk to you anymore, it seems they hate you so much for no apparent reason. What can you expect from a total stranger? Wake up, Dad, and put your mind to think a little."

I kept listening to her until she finished her lecture, then I hugged her and thanked her for her wise words. I should have listened to her right then and followed her recommendations. But I didn't, and that was the beginning of my troubles. I was exhausted because for the previous three weeks, I had worked long hours on my writing. By long hours, I mean an average of fourteen hours per day.

Margarita tried several times to take me away from the computer screen. I didn't pay attention to her because my fingers could not survive without tapping on the computer wireless keyboard. I was writing scenes and rewriting them about six times each until I was sure they were good enough.

Days turned into nights for those weeks, and soon I was on page 61, and on scene 65. One day, Margarita came to me, sad and crying. She asked me to take her out. Of course, I refused, for I had turned into a writing machine. I thought only about the main characters for the comic book and the screenplay, MegAm, and for a while, I forgot that I had a beautiful wife in need of time and care.

Anna was with me all the time because she was in love with the characters and didn't mind staying home with me. She stopped to check on the writing every half hour, and asked me the same question every time: "Are you done yet?"

To which I replied, "I've written one more scene than when you asked me the last time."

I was so busy that I didn't realize my last email had been intercepted and read by a fake agent who impersonated Stuart Stone. He had sent me the first email that day when he asked me to change the address that I already had on record.

He was very interested in me finishing the script, and he kept begging and pushing me to write it soon. As I said, I had been working hard and late for a while to finish MegAm. A few days after I changed the email, at about ten one night, I took a break. I stood up to stretch out my arms and legs, and I took a peek through the small window behind the computer. I saw a man's shadow opening the passenger door of my Honda CR-V, and the light flashed on.

I took off my glasses and cleaned my tired eyes. I looked again, after I put my glasses back on; I couldn't see anyone anymore. I sat back down on the chair, and that was the end of the mysterious moment. I thought it was a trick of my tired mind. I blamed a cat that came around every night and used to sleep under the van.

Two days later, Margarita forced me to take a break. "Mr. Revolori," she said, "I'm really angry and I'm going to send you away for good if you don't stop and give me a little bit of your time." Anna was watching and listening to the yelling. "Dad, the queen has spoken, and that's the end of it," she said and ended with clapping, "Bravo, bravo, and bravo!"

"Oh, boy!" I said, while Anna was still laughing and applauding.

Knus's words came back to my mind slowly, and I remembered our talk. He had seemed tired and took many long pauses before he cried, "I rightly deserve a long break, Mr. Revolori. I see you've been listening so patiently for quite a long time." He and I took a rest, and we saw that the light in the horizon already had foggy spots. We agreed that our time had to be cut short. All the park visitors had left, and the dark night was coming fast. I suggested we meet again the next day at noon to resume our conversation. He cleared his throat a couple of times. And he said in a slow voice, "I know it's getting dark, but it'll take me five minutes, ten at the most, to finish." Slowly, his voice faded away from my thoughts.

Stuart Stone sent me tricky emails twice a day, telling me that the script must be done in a week. He told me that he had close friends and connections with American producers living in Germany, and that they were interested in the project. I was very happy, and I sped up the writing, and soon I was on page 84, which was the last one I wrote that year.

That's how the nightmares for me with my long and trusted talent agent, Stuart Stone, started. He was ready to torture Anna, Margarita, and me. I believed the good shepherd owner of Stuart Stone Casting had begun to hate me and viciously attack me. Indeed, he had turned into a werewolf dressed in sheep's clothing. I didn't have a single clue that each day the light was turning into darkness. My talented precious daughter, my caring, beautiful wife, and I were about to be forced to go skydiving without parachutes.

I Met Stuart Stone

One day, at around two in the afternoon, Anna was getting ready for a callback audition. She spent a long time choosing what to wear and combing her hair in front of the mirror of her bedroom dresser. She came out to ask me about the tight blue jeans she had chosen. I said they looked good for the audition. She also asked me about her hair. I gave her my suggestion, and she chose to comb it into a high ponytail.

That afternoon we left the house early, and soon I was driving on the 110 Freeway. She tuned the car radio to her favorite radio station. She sang along with every song and asked me many questions about my favorite singers. At around three o'clock, we were passing by the skyscraper in downtown Los Angeles. At that point in time, I asked her to turn off the radio. She knew our daily routine when we drove together. We always split the time, half for listening to music, and the other half to do her homework. We always started with spelling, so this time I read big words from the building signs, and I spent fifteen minutes on the subject. I was so proud of her spelling abilities, and as always, she passed with a perfect score.

She answered all the questions in the spelling test that I had given her. It was time to switch to a different subject. I chose social studies for ten minutes, and science for five minutes. She was having a good time answering the questions, and she was passing them all, so I hit her with a very hard science question. "Honey," I said, "this is the last question, and if you get it right, we'll skip mathematics today." She yelled happily, and cheered herself up. She said, "Give me a high five for a pinky promise, Dad." Unfortunately, she didn't know the answer to the last question, and we ended up doing math, the subject that I hated to teach her. I have struggled with math all my life, and I have hated all number-related courses, all the way from elementary school to present time. We were close to taking the Santa Monica Boulevard off-ramp in Hollywood when she finished her schooling. She went back to listening to the radio.

We arrived at the casting building at 4:27 pm, walking into a packed audition waiting room. It was full of strange and unfriendly actresses who we later learned were casting for several porno videos. About thirty half-naked young porn actresses were bumping into each other, waiting for their nasty audition. Till then, I had literally been to thousands of auditions with my older sons, and I hadn't seen such unsavory characters in a well-known casting agency. About a dozen mothers were waiting for their kids to audition for the project Anna was hoping to book. I read their minds and their gestures. It was easy to guess they were very upset.

I was sitting with Anna on a long bench, and a gorgeous black actress came to sit next to me. She chose to sit on my left side. She smiled and said hi to me. She was seductive and provoking the sexual urges of all males in the room. We could see her naked breasts, and she had hickies on one of them. Her nipples were hanging down and even her vagina was almost visible because her bikini was so small that it didn't cover her properly. Anna was upset to be in that environment, and a mother with her teenage son sitting next to her, turned to me and shook her head.

Ten minutes later, Anna was escorted into the audition room. She came out twenty minutes afterward. I was already worried and irritated about the long wait. Usually, it takes five minutes for a long audition; the average time for auditions is two to three minutes. I was glad when Anna opened the door and popped up her head from the casting-only entrance door. She came out with a big smile and a happy face. She sat on the bench for a few seconds. I got up, took her hand, and pulled her. She hesitated to get up and pulled me down back to the bench. I was guessing what had gotten into her. Suddenly, she stood up and rushed out the door. I followed her not knowing why she was acting so strangely. I had parked nearby, and we walked to the car. While we were walking to the vehicle, she grabbed my hand, and still with a big smile on her face, told me, "Dad, I met Mr. Stuart Stone in person. He came to the audition room just to meet me, that's what he said."

I had seen him in pictures and videos, but I forgot to ask her what he looked like in person to make sure he was the right man. Anna told me that he was very nice. At that moment, I didn't know that both my life and hers were on the line. I just listened to her and shared her happiness. We walked to the car I had parked on the southbound side of Santa Monica Boulevard a couple blocks away from the casting office. I drove south for a few minutes down Boulevard, heading home. All of a sudden, Anna changed her mind and asked me if I could take her to Sam's Ash music store on Sunset Boulevard. I slammed my foot on the brake pedal to slow down. I made a left turn on the next small street, and a couple minutes later, I was driving on Sunset Boulevard. Soon, we were checking out guitars at Sam's Ash bass guitar department, and Anna played a few of them. After a while, she set her mind on a $700 Fender bass guitar.

My brain was still active, and it sent millions of questions to my mouth, one of them being, why had Stuart Stone met with Anna at the auditions? I could not figure it out, but my thoughts never gave me a break. The strange thing was that Stuart Stone said to Anna not to tell me that he had talked to her in somebody else's casting agency. When Anna told me about it, she mentioned three strange issues: first, that Stuart Stone told her that she had a killer body and great curves; second, that he went into the auditioning room in secret to meet her. He said to her that the casting director was his friend and allowed him to go in to talk to her. Third, he cursed and used vulgar language when he was chatting with her. According to Anna, he said, "These bitches are f—— hookers auditioning for porno videos."

Stuart Stone is a respected casting director and a top producer in Hollywood. I couldn't figure out how to solve the puzzle. The truth was that the casting director was playing dirty tricks on me. And Anna was in danger. I felt it in my heart, but my brain was blank.

Anna noticed that I was deep in thought, and with a kiss on my cheek brought me back to reality and happiness. She asked me, "Daddy, are you going to buy it for me tonight?" She answered her own question before I had enough time to reply to her, and she said, "I want this one, and I'm taking this baby home now." We went to the cashier and put it on a layaway plan that they offered me.

We left the store, and twenty minutes later we were southbound on San Pedro Freeway, passing downtown Los Angeles on the way back home. My cell phone beeped and vibrated to give me a text alert. Anna checked it and opened the inbox icon. She read the message to herself. It was an email from Stuart Stone.

"It is nice, but weird," she said, then hesitated for a second. After a long pause, she started reading it to me:

"Hello, Mr. Revolori, I saw you and your daughter today. My son and I went to Sam's Ash and saw you checking out bass guitars. We saw Anna playing a few of them. Don't worry we aren't following you or anything like that. I'm leaving for Germany tonight. My son is taking me to the airport. He asked me to take him to buy a bass guitar that he needed. It was by chance that I saw you and your daughter shopping there. It's nice that I bump into you everywhere. It's good luck, I guess. Don't you agree?" Anna stopped reading the text message. She saw the change in my body language, and asked me, "What's wrong, Dad?"

I gave her a fake smile to calm her down. I didn't want her worried about what I was thinking. I kept thinking, *Stuart Stone is following me, but why?* After a pause, I asked her to keep on reading the text. She cleared her throat, like imitating a good actress.

Stuart Stone wrote, "When I return from Germany, I'll get in touch with you again. Take a good care of Anna, please. Cheers." After she finished reading it, she turned the radio on and the volume up.

In the deepest recesses of my mind, I knew that I was very frightened. I forced myself to focus on good feelings, and to put wise words in my mouth. I was quiet all the way back to our house. Anna knew I was worried and didn't say a single word until we parked in the driveway. She ran inside, and went straight to the kitchen, and a few minutes later she handed me a hot, hand-squeezed lemon tea.

I went back to my writing and started to work on a new song. Anna asked me to let her watch "Bones", one of her favorite TV series. I worked hard to forget about the strange casting director's motives for following me, but I couldn't stop thinking for the next two days. The thinking was killing me. I desperately wanted to know why Stuart Stone was spying on Anna and me. I just knew one way to put my mind to rest: I prayed a lot, asking the Lord for protection, forgiveness, and blessings. As I said before, I don't associate with any religion, but I know I'm a Christian. I trust God, maker of heaven and earth, and the giver of life. To me, the Lord is an awesome, caring, and loving God.

Sing and Dance, Sashia

One afternoon, I received a very weird email from the Stuart Stone Casting office. The email was sent by Stuart Stone. It was a casting notice for an untitled project that they were going to shoot somewhere in Europe.

He wrote, "Hello, dear Revolori, you are a good friend to me. In fact, call me Stuart, I'm your best friend, and no longer Mr. Stone." He continued in the next paragraph: "I was checking your website, and I found out that you represent other artists. I saw a Mexican Native American girl among your talent. I'm casting a big project. I can't give you more details yet, but it is a huge project from Sony and Paramount Pictures. I'm interested in Sandy, the Native American girl you represent. She's a perfect match for what the producers are looking for." I was happy to read the email and that my actress was going to get picked for an unknown movie produced by two major networks.

I called Sandy's parents to ask them if she was available. Anna heard me and got sad and a little jealous. I explained to her that in life, opportunities come to everybody, and all we need to do is take advantage and open the door when they come. If they knock on the door, we let them in as fast as we can because it could be our only chance, and we can't afford to miss the boat. After Sandy's parents gave me the go-ahead, I contacted Stuart Stone and confirmed the tape audition.

He sent me about five emails that day. They kept changing the sites and the songs for the audition. Sandy was supposed to sing and dance in the movie. I went along with the casting director, but I was having a hard time with Simone, Sandy's mother. She was a very demanding woman. I don't blame her; she was just protecting her daughter. I must say, her father was cool, and he supported Sandy, but Simone had a different way of teaching her things, and I had to deal with her. Sandy didn't know a thing about singing or acting; she couldn't carry the melody, and needed to learn how to sing in tune. But the real challenge was Simone's attitude. They both thought—in fact, they were certain— that Sandy was the best singer and the best dancer ever, and yes, she was talented, very sharp, and a cute girl, but she needed intense coaching. On the other hand, Stuart Stone was pressing me and changing the deadlines, and he wanted me to tape her audition fast and upload it to Google Drive and send it to him right away.

I received three songs for Sandy to sing, and two for the dancing routine. I spent three days coaching her. Anna helped me to teach her the basics. We worked long hours rehearsing with her in both singing and dancing. The poor girl didn't have a clue nor training; all she did was move her body with the rhythm, and her singing needed a lot of coaching. The taping day arrived, and I did what I could to get her ready because we were taping the audition at 8:15 in the evening. The producer had requested a night shooting, according to Stuart Stone.

My cell phone beeped to alert me that an email was stored in the inbox. We were about to finish the taping with Sandy when the message arrived. I gave her a ten-minute break so I could read the email. My gut feeling told me I had to read it immediately. I was shocked when I read the first sentence. Once again, it was from Stuart Stone. The producers had changed all the songs but one, so all my work, and time had gone down the drain. I gave the troubling news to Sandy's parents, who were waiting in the small living room at my place. When they heard me saying, "We are going to change the songs, and we are going back to the beginning," Simone stood up. She grabbed her purse, and she gave me a look. Her husband was calm. He said, "Whatever we have to do, we are in."

Sandy and Anna heard our conversation. They came in storming into the living room and hit me with questions. I wasn't sure what to do. I just prayed for a solution to the problem. I remembered that an old friend, Theresa Dahlquist, a talent agent, and owner of Beverly Hetch Talent

Agency, once told me, "Remember, all problems have a solution. If you can't solve a problem, then the solution is you can't. In time, you'll forget it. But the next day you must clear it out of your mind."

In about ten minutes, I had charmed my girls and Simone. Anna made coffee, and we were eating cookies and laughing. We talked about the new songs and scheduled the days to rehearse the singing and dancing routines. Anna and Sandy were playing video games on a tablet. They were having a good time. And I was having a productive conversation with Sandy's parents.

The days went by, and I went to Sandy's house to rehearse the new songs, but she was not paying attention. It was so hard for Anna to teach and control her. Simone was always watching and correcting whatever we taught her. It seemed that she wanted to undo what we had done right. We worked Monday through Friday for two hours every afternoon, after school. Sandy and Anna were tired, but I was doing just fine. Sandy was getting better with the dancing routines, but her singing was still way off.

I informed the casting director about her progress. He answered, telling me not to worry about her singing because the producers were interested in her looks. And for the singing and dancing, she was going to be professionally coached if hired. The next email eased my concerns and frustration. I knew Sandy wasn't ready for the audition, not in my wildest dreams. Nonetheless, I had to tape it the next afternoon, which was a Saturday.

On the way home, Anna talked to me about the project. She said, "I'm sick and tired of dealing with Sandy. Dad, she doesn't listen, and Simone hates me." I felt her pain and sadness cutting to the bottom of her heart. She continued, "You should see the dirty looks they give me behind your back. One time, Sandy even gave me the middle finger. I don't want to work with them anymore."

I knew I had to come up with a Plan B to solve the conflict. Anna and Margarita meant the world to me. I wasn't going to let nobody tear my family apart. I called upon the Lord to show me the way, but I was running out of time. I promised Anna that I was going to tape the audition, send it to Stuart Stone, and drop Sandy. Anna agreed to my promise; she trusted me. I always kept my promises to her and to Margarita. I stopped at Baskin Robbins to treat her to an ice cream. She finished her banana split, and we went straight home. Margarita was waiting for us with Pupusas, our favorite food. She had them ready to be served. I was very tired, and I went to rest after I ate. I gave myself a break for the rest of the night. Anna went to her bedroom to watch TV. Margarita and I stayed in the living room, and we had a good and healthy conversation. We chose a movie on Netflix and watched it. I boiled water to make coffee for her and brought it to the sofa. Oh boy, I enjoyed that evening talking and watching movies with her. It was already midnight when we turned the television off and went to sleep. I couldn't catch up any sleep the whole night. I kept putting my plans together. I was sure I needed to drop Sandy. I was worried about Anna's future, and she made it clear I had to get rid of Sandy. It was already dawning, the sun was rising, and soon it was up shining bright in the middle of the sky. It's 9:11, a beautiful cold morning—that was the Saturday I was going to tape the audition.

I fell on my knees, and I gave thanks to my Father in heaven for a new day, and I asked for health, forgiveness, and for guidance on the matter. That same afternoon, we taped the audition. Anna and I worked very late because we had to cut it, edit it, and upload the video to Google to send it the next day to the casting director. The producers were pushing Stuart Stone, and he was pressing me to send it Sunday early in the morning.

Anna Is Booked Too

I sent the audition video to Stuart Stone, and the producers watched it as soon as they got it. He sent me an email that Sunday night a little after eight. He was so happy that the producers liked it. Anna was in almost all the scenes helping Sandy, so the producers had the chance to watch her dancing skills and hear her amazing voice.

I was ready to let Sandy go as I had planned. Margarita had to give me the okay to drop her, for she was a good friend of Simone's. In fact, I was representing her because Margarita and Anna had begged me to give her a chance. Anna and Sandy were best friends, according to them. I thought Margarita wasn't going to let me drop her. I had decided to go the next afternoon to speak to her parents to give them the news. I planned to tell them that it was for the best that I was going to let Sandy go. I even thought to help them out and give them a list of talent managers I knew in the Hollywood area.

About forty minutes later, Anna spotted a second email in the inbox. I opened it, and it changed the whole thing. Now, I needed to choose one from two pieces of bad news. I wasn't going to drop Sandy after all, because the producers wanted Anna to be in the movie too.

When Anna found out that the producers wanted to book her, she was very excited. I explained her that she was only going to be considered because the chemistry she had working with Sandy was very real. If they ended up booking Sandy, she might get the part too. They were interested in Sandy and wanted to book her. It happened that they liked the interaction when Sandy and Anna were singing and dancing together. They were very different physically, yet their chemistry was very unique when they performed. Anna was a tall, beautiful, slender, fair-skinned, talented singer, dancer, and performer. She was eleven years old, but mature and looked sixteen.

On the other hand, Sandy was eight years of age, a little full-figured, wild, dark-skinned, short, and of Aztec Mexican descent. In spite of the drastic physical differences, truly, they were amazing when they were on the stage. I had seen that they worked wonders; really, they were special performers.

The casting director and the producers had asked me to tape a second audition video. They said they wanted Anna to audition as Sandy's best friend, the one who teaches her singing and dancing in the movie. For the first time, they revealed the name of the project. They released the screenplay title, "Sing and Dance, Sashia." It was a feature film created by two major networks, Sony Pictures in collaboration with Paramount Pictures. They said they were interested in casting Anna for the role of Julia, which was the second leading role. Sandy was going to get the first leading role of Sashia, a girl who dreamed of becoming a pop singer and world-famous dancer ever. Her biggest challenges were that she didn't know how to sing or dance.

Anna wasn't happy when she found out that she was auditioning for the second lead role. Margarita and I had a hard time making her understand that little wheels turn big wheels. Finally, she accepted that this time Sandy was going to get the best role in the movie. She agreed to do her best in the audition tape and to work with Sandy.

I received five new songs in English, and two in Spanish to work with the girls for the second audition. I went into my home studio to prepare the rehearsals. In about three hours, I had already figured them out. I was ready to put pressure on the girls for five more days of hard work.

I rehearsed with them for three hours the first day; they learned a lot. Anna quickly mastered the dancing routines for the three songs. Sandy didn't show any progress or interest because she arrived from school already tired. She spent most of my valuable time talking and going to the bathroom. Every afternoon that week, we had to go to Sandy's house to rehearse, and Simone sat on the couch watching. Her presence made me uncomfortable and stopped me from getting the best from Sandy.

By the third day, Anna was complaining and fighting with Sandy. Simone was giving Anna hateful looks. I knew something nasty was going to blow up at any minute. I was mentally prepared from the first day we started the callback rehearsals. The tension was escalating by the second. I read Simone's gestures and body language. I was just waiting for her to get up and shoot us down with a single shot in the heart.

We finished the rehearsal at shortly after seven. Luckily, for us, Sandy and Simone hadn't attacked us yet. We had survived one more day. I felt that I was wasting way too much of my time for little to no respect or appreciation for my hard work.

The next day, I went to teach at Sandy's place again. It was the fourth day out of five that we had planned to coach her before taping the callback audition. About an hour and a half had passed. It was almost time to end it for the day. I took a long break and answered a few texts, including a couple from Stuart Stone. We went back to business fifteen minutes later. Sandy wasn't ready and told me, so I gave her another ten minutes' break. Simone was watching me closely, then got up and walked out the door. She went to her small retail store across the street.

I grew afraid because Sandy's house was located near neighborhood in South Central Los Angeles known for drug dealing and gangs. I followed her with my eyes while she was walking across the street. She gave high fives to shirtless black gangbangers standing on the street corner. At that moment, my heart felt as if a sharp knife was cutting deep into it. I honestly felt as if it was a warning from God.

I turned to look at Anna, and then I moved my eyes to Sandy. She noticed and gave me a challenging stare. I couldn't take it anymore. I said with a firm friendlyvoice, "Sandy, do you want to continue with this audition or not? I'm not going to waste my time if you don't want to pay attention. You must follow instructions, or we stop right now for good."

She replied quietly, "I'm angry, I don't want to do it anymore." Anna was just looking and biting her nails.

"Good then," I said. That's it! Let's go home, it's time to leave." We dropped Sandy off with Simone at the store. I told Simone that I wasn't going to represent Sandy anymore. She began to yell at me, but I controlled the urge to yell back and to defend myself. I answered her with a powerful voice, "Sandy doesn't want to rehearse anymore."

About a dozen gang members, both males and females, gathered around us as they cheered her on in support. They started to insult me. Sandy, Anna, and four of Sandy's siblings were watching. Sandy's older brother grabbed a baseball bat and got ready to swing. Of course, I wasn't going to let him hit and score a home run. I whispered to Anna, who was my best pitcher, to throw him a few low and high curveballs to strike him out. The game was over, and a couple of minutes later, we were walking out the door. Anna was okay, but she was very scared. That was the end of "Sing and Dance Sashia" for Anna and her best friend Sandy. I don't believe in best friends. I had been telling Anna and Margarita that there was no such thing. To me, my only true best friend is Jesus.

I hope and pray people who'll have the chance to read this inspirational true story book understand that Jesus is the answer, not friends or religion. Don't you ever give up your faith and hope. Always, carry on, and trust that He is there, ready to protect you when you ask for help. And at the end of each day, you'll get the victory. Jesus has done it for me time and time again. I'm not trying to sell any religion or change the way you are. God loves you just the way you are, but you need to be obedient to the Lord and keep his commandments.

I don't belong to a religion, but I have Jesus in my heart, and God the Father leads the way for me. He guides my soul and gives strength to my mind and heart to praise His name. I have suffered a lot throughout my life, but I'll be following Jesus until the day I die. And I will enjoy my life. I'll always love the Lord with all my heart. I also love music, which is the bridge between God and men. I'll care for my family, relatives, friends, and people around me, even my enemies. I'll share and give love, truth, faith, and forgiveness, even in tough times.

The Visitor

I had just stepped out of Sandy's store, and I was opening my car door when a message came in. I ignored it because I wasn't in the mood to read it. So, I drove off the curb and sped away. The message was sent three more times. I thought it was an emergency text, or it was extremely important and I pulled over to check it. Stuart Stone was urging me to reply to him as soon as I could. Immediately, I answered him. He texted me back and told me to go back home at once.

Now, I was certain he was planning something bad against Anna and me. I became so afraid of him that I couldn't control my emotions. I thought that Anna and Margarita were going to be kidnapped. He told me that he was waiting for me in my house. He added that he came to pay me a visit to give me a surprise in person.

I drove very fast and got home in twenty-three minutes. I was hoping to find the mysterious visitor waiting for me. I was breathing hard and unevenly. I felt as if my heart was going to explode and blow up the car I was driving. I was cruising so erratically that other drivers were honking at me wildly. Luckily, I didn't get pulled over and made it home safely. I found a couple of open parking spaces, and I parked under an orange tree. I walked around the back of the house.

I made sure no one was about, and I checked the windows, then I opened the door and went inside. I was relieved because everything was in place, the windows were locked, and nothing was missing. I went out and walked around the entire building to see if I could spot any suspicious activity. Everything was safe and secure…or so I thought. Anna was waiting for me inside. I went back in and told her the truth, and why I was worried, but I assured her that everything was fine.

My cell phone beeped again just when I was getting comfortable on the small sofa. Anna guessed right. It was Stuart Stone texting me one more time. It seemed that he was never going to stop bothering me.

I asked Anna a question. "What does he want from me?" My nightmares and suffering were getting worse.

Stuart Stone texted me, "Mario, I left your house twenty minutes ago. I waited for you for a while, but soon I found out you were at Sandy's place. I told my partners to go meet you there to give you the surprise. I just arrived here, but you and Anna were already gone. I tell you, what bad luck for all of us. We have a plane to catch in three hours. We're going to Germany again. The producers and I need to scout for locations. We really wanted to meet you and your daughter in person."

Meanwhile, three men walked into the grocery and toy retail store near Sandy's house. They looked around for a few minutes to check the place out. First, they tried to talk to Ciccio, but he refused to answer their questions. Then they spoke with Sandy's younger brother. They asked him a bunch of questions about their family members and their relationship with me. The boy was not aware that they were getting confidential information and he told them everything they wanted to know. They paid for a bottle of water and two Cokes and left.

The strange agent sent me another email informing me that he had the names of all of Sandy's family members. He said that the producers needed to make sure that everything was good, and they wanted to check all of us for criminal records before they booked Sandy for the role of Sashia. When he gave me this new piece of information, I grew afraid and started to feel a sharp pain in my chest. I took a deep breath to fill my lungs with fresh air. After a few minutes, I controlled my nerves a little. I wanted to go to the police, but I thought the casting director was only playing jokes on me.

I was about to tell him about the quarrel I'd had with Sandy and her mother, but I decided to wait. I tried to get some sleep that night, but it was almost impossible to quiet my mind and to tame my brain.

Next Day

I woke up very late the next morning. I was physically and mentally exhausted. I didn't want to get up because my legs were a little weak, and my stamina was failing. I couldn't stop thinking that I wanted to find out what was going on in Stuart Stone's mind. I didn't have any answers, however. Margarita and Anna got up and put some food on the table, and they called me to go eat. They noticed something was wrong with me. Margarita slid next to me. She gave me a big hug and a kiss. Tenderly, she wrapped her arms around me and asked me to tell her the problem. I took a big pause. Slowly, I spoke, and my hands were shaking as I told her that I was going to drop Sandy. I didn't mention anything about Stuart Stone's strange visit to our house. Anna mouthed me to tell Margarita about him. I mouthed back that it wasn't a good idea to tell her then.

The sun was up and the morning was speeding toward noon, and my head was spinning around. I hadn't found a solution to my troubles yet. First, I needed to tell Stuart Stone that Sandy was not my client anymore. I kept thinking what his reaction might be. Second, I needed to find out why he was spying on me. And finally, would he harm me? Was Anna in danger?

One thing I was certain of was that I could trust Jesus. It was already time to consult with him and trust in him, because he had never abandoned me in the past. And I always believed in him blindly, so I turned my fears over to him.

The sun began to drop in the horizon. I went to the backyard and sat on a wooden bench, underneath a fig tree. I decided to watch the sun setting, and fleets of huge airplanes were lined up in the sky. They kept approaching to kiss the ground on the majestic LAX runway. After I meditated for forty-five minutes, I knew it was time to do what I needed. I had already made up my mind.

I went back inside, and sat in front of the computer screen. I thought it over for a minute and thirty-eight seconds, directing my eyes to the keyboard. Gradually, I moved my right hand and placed my fingertips on the keys. My left hand followed, and soon I was writing a long paragraph to Stuart Stone. In a matter of minutes, I had finished it. I called Anna to proofread, to correct any mistakes and to add changes we needed to make. She read it over and made a few changes for me. I checked it again and hit the send command. My heart was pounding fast. Anna looked at me. All I had to do was wait for an answer from Stuart Stone. I hoped he would reply pretty soon. I was sure it wasn't going to be a pleasant answer.

I got a reply sooner than I ever imagined. He started his first sentence, cursing every word he wrote. I knew he was angry, almost going mad. I read the entire first paragraph. As I continued reading the next one, I became very afraid.

Immediately, I wrote to explain to him that Sandy and her mother had told me they were going to quit the auditions for the movie "Sing and Dance, Sashia." I tried to convince them to go on and told them that we were going to go separate ways after the audition process. They told me there was no way on earth that they would do such a thing. So, I wrote to Stuart Stone about it. He implored me to go and talk to them again and to start all over. I also received a phone call from Sandy's father telling me that he urged me to continue with the audition. He said he was going to talk to Simone to persuade her to change her mind. After he spoke with Simone and Sandy, he called me again to schedule a meeting with them.

The casting director also pleaded with me to set a meeting with them. He wrote, "I beg you to talk to them because the producers are bugging me. Anna and Sandy were the top two finalists to book the movie. The producers also reminded me that they were interested in Sandy only. They were considering Anna because the chemistry they have when they sing and dance together is unmatchable. They said that they needed Sandy because no one had her physical looks. But Anna could be replaced easily. I know that you're a smart man. You're Anna's manager, and you're her dad, and you care for her, but the producers were clear with me." He added, "One more thing: If Sandy is out, so is Anna, and we all kiss goodbye the chance they have to book this amazing film. In fact, this is the only opportunity they have to make it big. It is already in the books. They must not throw it away, don't be stupid."

The Meeting

The following afternoon, I spent several minutes thanking the Lord. I began to bless his name, and most importantly, to ask him to clear my mind. As always, after I prayed, the Lord heard me and showed me the way to go and to take baby steps to make my final decision to solve any problem. Now more than ever, I needed help from his mighty angels. This time, I was given wisdom and knowledge by my Creator to choose correctly. I finished my short interior spiritual conversation with the Lord, and I was ready to proceed.

I made a phone call to Simone. First, I apologized, even though I hadn't done anything wrong to her. I had learned through the years that people love apologies because they never accept that they are wrong. Many times, when aggressive drivers cut in front of me on purpose, I tell them my favorite phrase: "My fault, bro," I apologize. They nod, smile, and drive away happily. It works every time; it calms them down.

I have seen people pull out bats, knives, and guns when I have stood up for my rights. Nowadays, they don't see, nor do they accept the truth. Humanity is turning into a gigantic zoo. Everyone wants to be right, and nobody's wrong, because they close their eyes and cover their ears; they simply don't admit the truth. Going back to my healthy conversation with Simone, I was making progress with her, and I made an appointment to meet with her in an hour just after six. She agreed to meet with me on one condition. I had to bring Anna with me. Now I faced a problem, I didn't have enough time to make it in time. I had less than an hour left, and I needed to pick Anna up. I was shopping at a nearby store, and it was already after five. Fifteen minutes later, we jumped into the car and drove through small streets, taking shortcuts. I tried to avoid the highway. I didn't take the 105 Freeway because it is usually packed all the time, day or night. Finally, I arrived several minutes late. I walked in cheerfully, with a big smile on my face. Anna went to play with Sandy, who was standing with her big sister in the aisle. Sandy ignored Anna's hello and mouthed bad words at her in Spanish. Meanwhile, I said hi to Simone. I didn't hear any answer from her for a long time. I was ready to go, and the Advocate, the Holy Spirit comforted me in my troubles.

I waited a little longer, and I told her, "I'm sorry about yesterday; my most sincere apologies." She heard me and turned around very slowly.

Still angry, she said, "Yes, all the customers came to tell me that I should have kicked you out of my store. They would have done the rest to you on my call." I was afraid after hearing her answer, but I remembered that the Lord is my Shepherd, and even in the hell ghetto of South Central Los Angeles infected with drugs, prostitution, and gangs, the Lord my God, would save me. I was waiting for her to speak and give me an answer. I called Anna with a hand movement to come with me. I apologized to Simone one more time. I asked Anna to say sorry for the trouble we had caused her.

Anna looked at me, and whispered, "Dad, we didn't do anything wrong to them. Why do I have to apologize?" She added in a lower voice, "I have to say I'm sorry? There'sno way, Daddy. I'm not going to do it." Sandy came over with a defiant look.

She said, "Hi, Mario." I replied very politely with a warm hug. I'm always a good pretender, but my feelings were eating me up alive.

Within five minutes, black gang members started to arrive. Soon there were five of them inside the little store. There were four boys and one girl. I was on the lookout the whole time. I saw one of them looking at me. He was on his cell phone the whole time.

Three minutes later, a tall muscular shirtless black dude showed up. Apparently, he was the leader of the gang. He had three thick golden chains around his neck. He was wearing gold and silver rings on most of his fingers. He had a pair of bright colored shorts on hanging down to his upper legs. He noticed me and greeted Simone. I had the feeling they came because of me.

The gangbanger said, "My good lady, is this mother—— bothering you? I can put him away before the sun goes down and cast his dead body in the Pacific Ocean if you want."

Simone stared at me and gave me a sarcastic smile. She turned back to the shirtless man. She shook her head, and with a loud voice she said, "No, he's my husband's accountant."

The gangbanger replied, "I just wanted to make sure. My boys are my ears and my eyes around here. You're part of the hood too. I just want you to know that."

I took a deep breath of relief.

A minute later, a large Hispanic woman walked in. She was barely dressed, her pendulous breasts almost hanging out of her blouse. She was showing her butt, half covered and half-nude. She called out from the door in a loud voice, "Simone!" Simone turned and walked to greet her with a loving embrace.

The strange woman gave me a flirtatious look, and said to Simone, "Is this cutie pie your friend? Introduce him to me. He's kind of cute; I'm interested, and I'll take him home now." I lowered my eyes to the ground to avoid direct eye contact with her. She walked around the aisle to look for merchandise and left me alone. Simone asked Sandy if she wanted to continue working with me in the "Sing and Dance, Sashia" movie. Sandy just looked at me and shrugged.

I took advantage of the moment and told Simone, "I'm sure she's tired with school and the audition rehearsals. It must be hard for her. We'd better stop the whole thing, and I'll deal with the casting director and producers." I assured her that I cared about Sandy. I added, "We need to let her rest and not force her." Simone was happy to hear my advice.

She said, "That's what I told my husband, but he doesn't listen. He thinks only about money. He doesn't care about Sandy. He just wants to get the dough. I will work day and night to put food on the table for her, and also I'll take good care of her."

I tried to play it smart, and before I left, I told Sandy, "I'll see you later, crocodile. And don't forget you're the best in the west and better than Anna and me."

She giggled and corrected me. "It goes like this: 'I'll see you later, alligator. You're the best in the west and better than the rest.'" She added, "Mario, you're a teacher and you don't know it." I smiled and gave her a high five.

Anna waved goodbye. "Now you know teachers don't know everything," Anna yelled as she was walking out the door.

The whole time I was standing in front of Simone, I was praising the Lord in my mind so nobody heard me, because some people are so touchy to talk about God. I didn't mention to Anna that God had cleared my mind and filled my heart with love for them. I thanked Simone and turned to leave. I spotted one of Simone's older daughters wiping the statue of the Virgin of Guadalupe, set on top of a shelf next to the exit. Happily, I went home, knowing that I had solved the problem for good. Now the trouble was going to burst wide open with the casting director.

I did a lot of praying and meditation in the meantime. I set Plans A, B, C, and D before I notified him. I had no idea that a month later, I was going to find out that my plans hadn't worked. I had been dealing with the Beast the whole time, and not with the real Stuart Stone from Stuart Stone Casting. He had been impersonating the real

Stuart Stone for the last three months. And, he had been hunting me down for a long time to cut me in pieces. Perhaps he had been paid a lot of money to torture me physical and psychologically, and not just to kill me fast.

Anna and Margarita at Lucile's Restaurant November 14, 2016

Hacking

Stuart Stone was so angry that he sent an army of demons to follow me. He ordered them not to kill me, but first to torment me in body and mind.

One morning, I was driving northbound on the 405 Freeway a little after six. Anna was sleeping in the passenger seat. About ten minutes later, I was on the 101 Freeway going to Santa Barbara. I was taking her for a Sketchers commercial shooting.

I received a phone call, and was sure it was from Stuart Stone. He knew where I was at that exact minute and second. He told me that God had told him in a prayer where I was. Everything was out of control; I was in panic, and I feared for my life. I stretched out my right hand to reach for Anna's hand. I started to pray out loud.

Soon she joined me, and we made a special request. In a deep prayer, we asked the Holy Spirit to save us. I said to Anna that Stuart Stone had been spying on us for a long time. She noticed that I had been shaking and mumbling the words.

She asked me, "Is Stuart Stone going to kill you, Dad?"

I took hold of her, saying, "God is with us, sweetie." I took my eyes away from the lane, and I veered to the right and to the left lanes. The driver on the right lane honked and gave me the middle finger. I hit the brakes, and the car that was tailgating me almost rear-ended me. Angrily, he sounded the horn about five times. They kept looking at me with anger on their faces.

I gave them the sign of peace with my left hand and mouthed them my magic words, "I'm sorry! It's my fault." They smiled as soon as they read my lips. All of them nodded and sped away. I made sure Anna was fine, and I slowed down the rest of the way. I understood that I needed to concentrate and pay more attention on the driving.

I was letting my imagination wander around for a few seconds without taking a hand off the steering wheel. Suddenly, like a rocket, my brain clicked. I said it in a loud, almost screaming voice: "I— I have been hacked." And the hacker was no other than Stuart Stone.

Anna got scared and yelled, *"What?* Holy Christ! What are you talking about, Dad? You're a genius! You just solved the puzzle."

I shared with her that I was sure that Stuart Stone had installed a tracking device in my Honda 2016 CR_V. Now it was clear in my mind that he had been following us for quite a long time. The first thing that occurred to me was the time he was spying on us at Sam's Ash on Sunset Boulevard in Hollywood a couple of months before. Anna was very nervous and started to cry. I let her know that I'd protect her even with my own life.

We made it to Santa Barbara University campus, where the production company was waiting for us. We arrived about forty- five minutes early and went to get some drinks and breakfast from the production catering truck.

It was a long day. The director asked me if I could stay to finish a scene they couldn't get to on time. Finally, they wrapped after six that evening, and we headed back home. I did hit some heavy traffic, and there were a couple of accidents that slowed us down. One accident had some casualties— the ambulance and paramedics were picking up bodies, among them one was wrapped in white blankets. We assumed they had used the blankets to cover a dead body. It wasn't easy to make it back home.

Anna was starving to death, and she needed to use the bathroom. We couldn't move an inch for an hour. It was heading for eight thirty already; exhausted, thirsty, hungry, and sleepy. All of a sudden, the cops cleared the scene and gave us the right to go. Luckily, I had been waiting in the middle lane, and only one car was in front of me. I was glad the wait was over. From there, it took me twenty-one minutes to make it home.

The phone beeped the moment I put the key in the keyhole to open the front door. I turned the key and opened it. I didn't bother to check the phone because I knew where the email was coming from. Anna took my cell phone out of my front pocket and handed it to me to read the message. She read it with me, and she got scared. Stuart Stone was cursing me for not taping the audition.

Anna said very slowly, "He's threatening you, Dad. We must do something."

I replied, "Yes, honey, we should report this to the police. We'll talk to Margarita, and together we'll make a decision to file a report or not."

The next day, I received an unwanted image of a nude woman in the first email Stuart Stone sent me that day. I opened the next mail and the attachment, an erect penis, appeared on the screen. I saw the photo and read the message he had written underneath the picture.

He started asking me the following question: "Do I have a big d—— or not? Believe it or not, it is my own d——, and I want to know from you if it's average or huge." It felt like I read it at the speed of light. I turned my head around to see if Anna was anywhere near the computer screen. I closed the tab and put the computer to sleep. I walked to our bedroom to tell Margarita about it. Anna was watching "Bones," her favorite show.

I went in, sat next to Margarita, and massaged her upper back a little bit for a few minutes. I didn't say a word; I waited for the next commercial break to tell her what a dirty email Stuart Stone had sent me. Margarita and I went to the computer, and I showed it to her. I asked her to tell me what steps to take on the matter. She warned me that Anna was trying to overhear our conversation from her room. Margarita changed the subject and yelled to Anna to get ready to go eat out.

She answered back with a loud, "Yeah!"

Days went by. The emails came three to five times a day. Stuart Stone sent me all kinds of porno videos and links, which I deleted as soon as I received them. In his emails, he kept trying to force me to join him in watching porno videos and movies. He attached several links of the best porno sites in the world, according to his messages. I refused to comply with all his requests, and I tossed to the trash the junk mail he had sent to saturate my inbox.

He watched me all the time for the next two weeks. He followed me everywhere I went at any time. Luckily for me, he made a big mistake and asked me for my Facebook account and the password. I replied to him that I couldn't give him my personal information. He had the nerve to let me know that he knew it anyway. He said he just wanted to make sure it was the right one.

He also told me that he had been using it for past two weeks, but it was for work-related reasons only. He said, "You don't have to worry just trust me."

That day, I found out he was hacking my old Apple computer. Anna and I did a thorough search for cameras and devices installed in our Honda van, but we didn't find a thing. I had a long conversation with Anna because I just knew we were in big trouble. The emails kept coming, and I answered every single one. He wasn't aware that I was already working on the case to get rid of him.

The previous week, we made several incredible discoveries: (a) he was watching us on the television set; (b) every time we turned on the computer, he had a tracking device to see and read my emails; (c) he could hear our conversations and read messages on both Margarita and my cell phones because he had downloaded applications to track us on the phones; (d) a tracking system was installed in the car to follow me; and (e) hidden cameras were installed outside, and inside my apartment. After I made these shocking findings, I told Anna and Margarita to keep it a secret, and not to tell anyone about the casting agent's threats.

Threats

Stuart Stone sent me pictures of three German prostitutes from Frankfurt, Germany, and asked me to pick the hottest one. I didn't give him any feedback in the reply that I wrote him back. I completely ignored the subject of the hookers. He got mad; he was furious because I didn't mention which one was the sexiest. I received a nasty email from him. He told me that I needed to take a better care of Margarita and Anna or else God was going to punish me severely.

This was the fifth time he had mentioned that he had been getting divine revelations from God about my future catastrophic life. I knew he was lying. But he wanted me to believe that God had told him in dreams, revelations, and prophesies. He added that all of his dreams were going to come true in a few days. I replied in one of my emails that I trusted my Lord, and I didn't believe God had shown him any divination because God always gave me revelations, visions, prophesies, and dreams directly. This time I gave him a defensive answer. I had the guts to stop his evil plans and confront him.

He told me that Anna needed to watch Disney TV shows every night from seven to ten, Monday through Friday for two weeks. And she had to answer the surveys at the end of each show. He tricked me the first two days. Anna watched all the shows that he had requested. The second day it came to my mind that he was watching her on our own TV screen.

Anna stopped watching the shows on the third day. Stuart Stone wrote me an email eleven minutes after the show started. To my surprise, he was friendly and understanding that Anna wasn't watching the first show yet. I answered and dropped a bombshell. Kindly, I let him know that Anna was not going to watch the shows anymore because she had migraine headaches. Of course, I was lying to prepare myself with a good plan. He understood and begged me to make sure she'd watch the shows the next day to catch up.

According to Stuart Stone, the owner and producer of Hollywood Records, Robert Dawser, had already scheduled an interview to meet with Anna in three weeks for a music and acting audition. And Anna needed to be ready with the acting skills required by Disney's shows because they wanted to sign her to a singing and acting deal. It was part of the requirements for an exclusive acting and singing three-year contract with the Disney Group. He also told me that the Sony Group had contacted him for an audition, but we had to wait and focus with Hollywood Records' live audition that we were already waiting for.

Anna did not watch the shows the next day. This time, he sent me a text on the phone and angrily wrote, "What the hell is going on?" I asked him how he had found out that Anna wasn't watching the shows. He got mad and barked like a dog infected with rabies. He replied, "You shouldn't worry how I know, if you care for your daughter's education. You should support her and your wife if you love and care for them.

"Anna is ill, and soon you'll lose her if you don't take care of her. I promise, if something bad happens to her or your wife, I'll chase you like a rat. You won't find a hole to hide. I'll find you. I swear, I'll choke you and break your neck with my own hands." He continued, "God told me last night your daughter was sad because you mistreated her and she almost fainted. You'd better let her do whatever she wants. You have to give her three to five hours to spend on the internet every day, so she can watch any show or program she wishes. She can even watch pornography. It's better that you let her watch good porno sites now than if she does it herself later. I already sent you some amazing sex video links, and I will email you more. This isn't a game; comply with my demands or die for not obeying. I mean it, and remember, take good care of your daughter and your wife. God is watching you, and he talks to me in my dreams. I'll talk to you later."

I got very nervous, but now I was certain he had cameras on the television set and the computer, and he was watching us when the devices were on. I told Anna and Margarita not to turn on the television or the computer. We had to use the computer only for important messages. We didn't switch on the computer or watch TV for three days. He couldn't see us, but he was still listening to our voices on the mobile phones. I was sure he could still track us when we drove our Honda van.

He wrote me a friendly email apologizing for his bad behavior. He pleaded with me to tell him about my PMH. He said that he must know because he had met my sons from my previous marriage. He had spoken with them, and he learned that they hated me and hadn't answered my calls for more than three years. He told me to visit them, and he ordered me to ask them to forgive me for all the trouble I had given them in the past. He had their cell phone numbers and their physical addresses and gave them to me.

I replied, "I know my sons don't want to see me, but I love them. I have sent them many messages and emails already, but they never return my calls or emails. I pray for them three times every day. I forgive them, and I ask them to forgive me for my mistakes. I hope that they enjoy a happy and healthy life without me. They can visit me at any time or call me if they need a dad, a friend, a brother, or spiritual guidance at any time day or night. They can count on me 24/7 when they need me and wish to lean on me. I'll be here.

"They know about my health. They are aware I have been dying bit by bit, and my heart has been broken since the day I was born. If you really want to know, here is my medical record chart." I continued, "When I was a child, I had a major stroke, and I became a quadriplegic. I spent close to five moths dying on a handmade cot without a mattress in my village, in a straw hut in the hills of Guatemala. I remembered my dad used to roll my motionless body three times a day. The doctors said I didn't have a chance to make it, but my faith saved me because I trusted in the Lord more than the doctors' medical knowledge. God never fails us, physicians do. Within a two-year period, without drugs or medical help, I was running.

'The miracle boy', good people in my village chanted when I ran barefoot in the dirt and along muddy roads. I was back on my feet having fun with my brothers and sisters. I didn't have any friends because they disliked me. Adults hated me for some reason that I never knew.

"In my twenties, I suffered a second stroke; this one left me paraplegic for a long time. I sat in a wheelchair for a year. I had faith in the Lord that he was going to cure me as he had done when I was a little boy. I refused to seek medical support. The doctors set a time to fry my brain in an unnecessary brain surgery. They encouraged me to allow them to cut a T-bone steak from my lower back because I had a dislocated disc, according to them. To both requests, I said no, and I didn't take any pharmacy-prescribed medicine. At that time, I was already working on my BA. I never stopped, and even when I was still in a wheelchair, I took classes. Two semesters after the stroke I went back to California State University, Fullerton, to pursue my education. I had a complete, speedy recovery. And once again, I was back working two years later. I was active in sports, and I became a licensed recreational soccer and basketball coach. I got married in 1992, and two years later my first son was born. In four years, I fathered two sons and started my accounting business, and I owned a Mexican Restaurant.

"I wasted no time with my sons and gave them the best education, care, and love all of us parents must provide to our children.

"They went to the best public and private schools in Orange County. I was a former teacher, and I tutored them myself. I spent thousands of dollars in music, arts, and sports lessons, both private coaching and sport clinics. I educated them spiritually with Bible studies three times a week. No disrespect for their mother, but I was a father and a mother for them. I even did the cooking. I cooked for them twice a day, and the third meal we ate out at fancy restaurants. I took special care for them. I paid famous acting coaches, including Cynthia Bain and Gary Spatz, who had coached Justin Timberlake, Britney Spears, and Ryan Gosling. They took private lessons with well-known vocal coaches; among them Steven Memel, whose credit is coaching and helping Adam Levine from Maroon 5.

"On July 31, 2008, I had a third major stroke; this particular one was strange. My right side was paralyzed from my toes all the way up to my neck, then it switched to my left side and paralyzed me from my neck to the top of my head. As usual, it was a routine for me not to trust medical doctors. They ran all the tests and said that, according to their findings, I wasn't going to be able to walk again. I refused to believe them, and I was sure God was going to heal me soon.

I did physical therapy myself, and I used the old method of curing with natural remedies, exercising, eating healthy food, and spiritual healing by praying ten to twenty times a day. It was easy for me because I was used to praying a lot for as long as I can remember. I have to admit, I got spiritual and physical support from my twelve-year-old younger son, Tony, and from Ronnie, one of my brothers. My older son Mario Jr. didn't care that much about my deadly illness or my recovery. Again, by praying a lot and believing in miracles, I beat all the odds and within eight months, I was already taking steps.

"Time went by fast, and soon I started to raise my two boys the best way I could. On December 24, 2010, on Christmas Eve, my third son was born. I spent every minute teaching him and singing to him many times each day. I knew that I had to take good care of him. My wife started to cheat on me, and she didn't care for him, so I was a dad and a mom for my little boy too. My two older sons told me they would never leave me because I was the best dad in the world. But in September 2012, my older son turned eighteen and he went his own way and never spoke with me again, just because I tried to keep him out of trouble. On April 28, 2014, my middle son, Tony, also turned eighteen, and he sent me an email. He wrote me, "I want my freedom, I'm eighteen now." He kicked me out of a business I had started with them. I ended up heartbroken and sleeping on the streets."

I assured Stuart Stone that I had shared with him the truth about my life. And I ended with, "Now you have more information to judge me. They kicked me out of their lives and let me crawl like a snake. I begged them to let me visit my baby son countless times, but they and their mother refused to let me see him. Instead, they threatened me. They didn't have mercy on me. Of course, I made mistakes as a father, as a friend, and as a big brother. But one thing I'm sure of: I didn't deserve to be treated like an animal by my own sons and my ex-wife. I want you to know that I love them, I forgive them, and I ask them to forgive me, so tell them that. I'll talk to them if they need my help, but I will never trust them again nor have any close relationship with them. I pray to the Lord for blessings and success. I will live my life in peace and let them choose their own way.

"They can choose the right way if they wish, or go the wide path, which is almost everybody's choice, but leads to trouble. I love and respect them, but I don't care about them anymore. Now you've found out everything you wanted to know about me. I will pray for them day and night, for the rest of my life. I promise, and I will keep this promise."

The next morning, at shortly after eight, my email alert beeped. It was Stuart Stone replying to my long email. He wrote a long answer in a single paragraph, saying, "You have suffered a lot, for sure you have. Be ready, because you are going to suffer another stroke very soon. I see you in the hospital room dying. You are going to have a massive stroke in a few days. God told me that you are not taking a good care of your daughter and your wife, and I'm going to send you to the hospital to die. I'm going to put you in the hospital because I told you not to scold Anna and not to argue with your wife. Let them go free and let them do whatever they want. I have been watching you. I order you, call your sons as soon as possible. I already gave you their cell phone numbers. Also, I gave them your address and phone number. By the way, I want to know why you changed your Facebook account password. I tell you, if you treat them well from now on, God will forgive you. And you may not have a stroke if you do as I tell you.'

My immediate reaction was to send him an answer back. I wrote him the following: "I need to educate Anna, and if she doesn't obey, I have to put her in time-out. It's my responsibility to raise and educate her the best way I can. Margarita and I dream of a healthy family, and we will do everything in our power to save Anna. No one is going to tell me how to raise my own daughter and how to save my family from all the trash out in the real world, and I'm not letting them go wild in the dirty streets.

"You tell my sons it was their choice to kick me out of their lives; now I live happy with Margarita and Anna."

He replied with a short email to tell me that he was just joking about the whole thing.

FBI

Anna and Margarita started to weep and I wanted to protect them from Stuart Stone's threats. Margarita suggested I call the police to make a criminal report and to get protection. Anna was just shaking and scared. I asked them to write down any idea had so we could make a wise decision. Margarita called her best friend, Renee, to ask her if we could send Anna to play with her seven-year-old daughter, Marlene. Anna was jumping up and down with happiness. She loved to play with her little friend next door, and they used to play twice a week. She got her toys and ran out the door. Margarita stopped her for a minute to lecture her. She gave her two hours to play.

It was clear Margarita was worried and wanted to speak with me alone. She knew we were in deep waters, and her main concern was Anna. We sat on the couch, and she made herself a cup of coffee and a hot fresh ginger tea with natural organic honey for me. We talked for two hours about the emails and the threats that I was getting from Stuart Stone. Meanwhile, Anna was having the time of her life with her little friend. She had already forgotten the threats we were receiving. We didn't have any idea how dangerous that guy was. But I relaxed, knowing she was fine and happy at Marlene's place. I still feared that Stuart Stone could target Anna and hurt her. Margarita finished her cup of coffee and got up to pour a second one. She brought a piece of cake for herself and a plain croissant for me. I thanked her, but I didn't touch the bread. She said that when she was nervous or worried, she couldn't stop eating, and drinking coffee.

Jokingly, I said, "Honey, don't drink a third one because you will snort, and you will release lots of dirty air tonight. I don't want to sleep with noises or smells from my precious and sexy wife." I told her that I needed to keep my energy to run away from Stuart "broken bone" Stone. Margarita smiled and said she hoped the police delivered justice.

I tried to cheer her up with humor. "I forgot you never fart, sweetie, all the flatulence and smelly gasses are mine," I ended.

Christmas time was around the corner. We walked out to pick up Anna, and we took a Canon-EPS camera to take pictures of the Christmas lights from the neighbors' homes. We went inside Renee's house to chat with her for a few minutes. That was the idea, although I knew Margarita was going to have a long gossiping talk with her friend. I was prepared, and took my cell phone fully charged. I also made sure to bring a notebook and a couple of pens to write new ideas that I might have about MegAm. I just knew it was going to be a long wait. I listened to their conversation that lasted one hour and forty-five minutes. Finally, I told my wife that I was sleepy.

Anna and Marlene heard me and spoke, at the same time, voicing their objection. They yelled in harmony in high-pitched tones, "Playing, playing, more playing, we want."

Ten minutes later, we were out on the street heading home. Margarita changed her mind and decided to check all the Christmas lights in the neighborhood and Anna posed for a picture. We got a few good shots and went back home. We uploaded the pictures to the computer, and we picked the best three. We did some retouching and loaded to Anna's commercial Facebook account. The pictures went viral in a matter of minutes all over the world. Obviously, Stuart Stone saw them and wrote a nice comment. He also emailed me to congratulate Anna.

Anna got mad when Margarita lectured and scolded her because she hadn't done her math homework yet. It was ten at night, a little too late already. Clearly, it was time to get ready to sleep. She didn't listen to her mother. She was kind of ignoring her, and she was rude. I stepped in to make sure she obeyed. I spoke firmly, and my gestures did the talking. I pointed to the homework paper. She dragged her feet a few steps as she came to fetch the pages, then stretched out her arm and grabbed them. She had a pencil, a calculator, and a pencil sharpener in her left hand. She got so angry that she was shivering and shaking. For a split second, I forgot about the hacking and tracking.

At that point, I barely remembered the whole mess with Stuart Stone. I did not even think that he was watching me all the time. I wasn't aware that he was an impostor, a criminal on the loose.

The alert beeped on my cell phone, bringing my mind back to him. Margarita and Anna spoke at the same time, saying, "It's Stuart Stone for sure." I turned to them and nodded.

He wrote the following nasty threat, "I saw what you did to my girls, and I am pissed off. That will have drastic consequences. I'll send you to the hospital very sick, and you'll die there. God just told me that you are abusing and mistreating Anna and your wife. Anna is crying and shaking. Don't you see you're hurting them? That's it. I won't give you more chances."

I got into bed to get some sleep, but I couldn't fall asleep. I got up after eight the next morning. I sat in front of the computer. Anna moved a folding plastic chair next to me. I already knew what I was going to do about Stuart Stone's threats. When Anna was a little girl, she spent hours watching trash videos online. Margarita was a teacher and had a laptop, a desktop computer, and a tablet at home. She had a nanny to take care of Anna because I wasn't living with them to care for her. Anna used to trick the caregiver and got her hands on the devices to search for trash videos. When I found out that Anna was wasting her time and poisoning her mind, I thought I could still save her. I came up with a plan and passed it on to Margarita. She agreed with me. She resigned from her teaching job and moved to Anaheim, California, to live with me.

One evening, I sat down with Anna and Margarita, and together we chose the programs we were going to allow Anna to use. I asked Anna what educational software she would like to start with.

She loved music and acting, so she replied, "Pro Tools and Final Cut." I was surprised, and soon we bought the programs for her. Three months later, she was recording, mixing, and mastering original songs and editing short films. Later, she picked a bunch of courses in computer coding at Khan Academy. She studied many new applications. She mastered them, and she learned a lot about hacking and tracking. She had a lot of knowledge to help me break the codes. I asked her if she could check the computer for tracking devices.

She giggled, then she said, "I'm sure I can, Dad. Close your eyes, please. I'll break the codes now." She typed some magic numbers, letters, and symbols. She stopped for a second to crack her fingers. She looked at me and told me to open my eyes. I had them opened the whole time, she noticed. She took a big breath and yelled, "You're a cheater, Dad." She celebrated with her arms up in the air. Then I gave her a pinky handshake.

It was December 14, 2016, at 9:04 in the morning. Anna told me that Stuart Stone had installed tracking and hacking devices on the desktop Apple Lion computer, on the two LG cell phones and in the Honda CR-V. I asked her if she could deactivate everything from the computer data system. She was so busy typing codes that she didn't answer me. She just snapped her fingers, and in a minute, she had deactivated all the devices.

In a matter of seconds, the FBI got the information. We were still on the computer when a message came in from the Federal Bureau of Investigation office in Los Angeles. They notified me that they had blocked all tracking systems from the Honda, the two LG mobile devices, and the Apple Lion computer.

They told me that we were safe for 780 hours. I was sure Stuart Stone was going to find out that I had filed a criminal report against him. The day was gone; it was a dark night, and it was time to go to sleep. I was getting comfortable in bed still thinking about the tracking, hacking, and threats from Stuart Stone. All of a sudden, I received an email, and yes, the sender was Stuart Stone. I was afraid to read it. Finally, I calmed myself down and glanced over the lines.

He just asked me, "Why did you block me?"

The Lord was on my side. I felt I was the luckiest man in the world because he didn't know yet that I had filed a criminal report, and the FBI was monitoring and following him. There was still one way he watched me, and that was the TV, and a hidden camera he had installed inside my apartment. Every time Margarita and Anna turned the TV on, he could see us, and was able to hear our voices. From December 15 to 17, he ordered me to keep the TV on. I didn't do what he wanted me to do, so he stopped messaging me. Anna, Margarita, and I got a break, and freedom for a short time. We thought Stuart Stone's threats were over, and we relaxed for a while. Sadly, the worst was yet to come.

Prophetic Revelation

I was having a good time teaching Anna singing, dancing, and writing. It was December 16, a peaceful night. We had almost forgotten about the hacker. We thought that we had gotten rid of Stuart Stone. Now, we should be enjoying life. We talked about the next year's resolutions. Anna asked me for some Christmas presents. She wanted a Fender electric bass, and a Pearl Export New Fusion five-piece drum set. She already had a brand- new digital piano, a Yamaha keyboard, two guitars, and one Ibanez bass guitar.

Anna yawned a couple of times. She came to me for a hug, and I gave her a kiss on her forehead, on her cheeks, and one on her nose. But this night she didn't want to go to sleep before she received a big hug from Margarita. In the past, she seldom got kisses and hugs from her, so she was used to go to bed without having much love from her mother. It was her turn to say a prayer that night. We always took turns to lead our prayers before we went to bed, and in the morning when we got up. After we were done with our prayer, she went to give Margarita a good night kiss. I followed her all the way to her bedroom. Then, I went to put my pajamas on, and I had a short talk with Margarita. I did not tell her about the emails I had received from the FBI because I didn't want her to worry. I gave her a good night kiss. She fell asleep within minutes. I took at least forty-five minutes of stretching and turning before I got some sleep. I had a short nap and woke up with a painful migraine headache. I got up to take a painkiller, then went back to bed, hoping to get more sleep, but it wasn't possible. The headache became less severe within several minutes. I got up a second time to check on Anna to make sure she was okay. I went into her room and turned the light on; she was asleep. I flipped the switch off and walked out the door. I decided to check the computer for new emails. I didn't see any from Stuart Stone.

There was a bunch of spam and promotional emails, which I put in the trash and deleted for good.

It was one in the morning. I had just slept about thirty minutes, and I was very sleepy and tired. But the thoughts kept bouncing in my brain, and I couldn't control the sad emotions. I walked to my bedroom with my head hanging. I felt beaten. I couldn't sleep, but I was drowsy. I stayed in bed for another hour, but there was still something bothering me, because I was thinking about the threats from Stuart Stone. I tried to come up with a solution. I forced my brain to give me a reply, but even my brain was sick, tired, and slow to respond. A sweet voice came to my mind and gave me hope. My soul flew upward, and my spirit rejoiced. The voice gave strength, peace, and love to my flesh and spirit. My happiness brought me to the living room. The light came through the window; it was enough for me to see around. I was between a rock and a hard place. I looked for things to do for a minute. I got up from the sofa I was sitting on, reached for the light switch, and turned it on. I took a few steps back and ended between the sofa and the coffee table. My Bible was on top of the coffee table. At that moment, I knew I needed to pray and ask my Creator for spiritual strength and guidance.

My heart urged me to get on my knees to thank, to praise, and to ask my Lord Jesus for divine protection. I knelt down on the tiled floor. It was the morning of December 17, 2016. The time was already 2:09, on the sixth day of Christmas. I had a long spiritual connection with Jesus, and I prayed for a long time with tears falling. My heart was pounding, and for a moment I believed it was going to burst from my chest. I began to sweat, and my whole body was soaked in salty water. At first, I got so hot I felt like I was on fire. Then, I became cold; the chills, and shivering never stopped. I was freezing. I prayed more. Nothing could stop me from praising God and blessing his name. Suddenly, a moment of peace, relief, and silence came to me and relaxed me physically and spiritually. The presence of Jesus approached me. My heart was at ease, my soul was chanting, and my strength was boosted from my tired brain and through my beaten body. Jesus was in total control of my body, mind, and spirit. He put a voice in my mind, and I listened to it. Everything was crystal clear; I just let the Holy Spirit guide my mind and my hands. Finally, I raised my hands up with my eyes closed so tight. I heard the Spirit of God telling me what he wanted me to know about the future. Especially, the torture I was going to face for the next eleven months. I stretched my arms and my hands ended on the Bible. A strong heavenly force controlled me. I opened the Bible randomly and stuck my fingers onto the page with my eyes shut. The Holy Spirit took me to the book of Ezekiel, then I opened my eyes and I read chapter 5 to chapter 7. Time had moved slowly, but it seemed to me that I had been praying for hours. I finished reading the first two sentences. I got sad, and my body weakened until I was about to faint.

I started on chapter 5, where it reads as follows:

> Therefore thus says the Lord God: See I am coming at you! I will inflict punishment in your midst while the nations look on. Because of all your abominations I will do with you what I have never done before, the like I will never do again. This means that fathers within you shall eat sons, and sons shall eat fathers. I will inflict punishments upon you and scatter all the remains of your people in every direction. (Ezekiel 5:8–10)

I was certain that God was speaking about my broken relationship with my two sons. And God wanted me to know about the madness going on around the world. It was a revelation that He wanted me to know ahead of time. I realized that I needed to change my lifestyle. I was praising the Lord night and day, but I had a problem: I was letting the wives of three of my best friends and clients flirt with me. Not only that; I did not stop girls in their early twenties trying to seduce me. Some of them even provoked me openly by sending me kisses and talking about how they would love to have sex with me.

For these and other sins, the Lord was angry with me, but saved me from losing my soul. I know now that I was chosen to praise and listen to the Lord when I was a little boy, and faithfully I would follow him for the rest of my life. God rescued me and washed away my sins that night because I hadn't had sexual relationships with any of the girls that Satan had introduced me to. But it was just a matter of time before I ended up in bed with one or all of them. I was sinking deep into moving sand. I blessed the Lord, for he came to me and pulled me out of hell. The road ahead of me was going to be tough. I was ready to drink the bitter cup, but I wasn't going to fail this time. I was drenched in sweat and tears, but at the same time, I was convinced that I had to suffer to save my dear wife and my precious daughter. I had already lost my three sons. I wasn't going to give up on my girls. The devil tried to trick me. He was sending me evil thought, and showing me the pleasures of sex, and material possessions. I remember how much I struggled to listen to my heart and to tell my mind to stop thinking evil thoughts. But I forced myself to only heed to the ones that were good, to follow the light, to see clearly what I had to face later on the very same day. It was amazing how every piece of information Jesus put in my mind came to pass. I never stopped praying and weeping. At last, I opened my eyes and checked the time on the stove's timer. It was 3:30 that Saturday morning, December 17, 2016.

I wrote down the time, the day, and the date on top of page 976 of my Bible. I put it on top of the coffee table and went to bed to catch some more hours of sleep. At 7:15, I got up and boiled a pot of rosemary tea, but Margarita didn't let me drink it for she wanted me to take her to do the laundry right away. I begged her to wait five minutes for me so I could drink it. She got very angry, went out, slammed the metal screen door, and waited for me in the car. Anna went with us to the laundromat. I didn't think that it was going to be the last thing I enjoyed that morning, and the last time that I was going to spend with my two ladies for the rest of the year, and for the rest of my life. Neither they nor I ever imagined that death was waiting to get the best of me.

Margarita and me at Lucile's Restaurant, Brea, California, November 14, 2016

With Anna at Lucile's Restaurant Brea, California, November 14, 2016

Rosemary Bush

Before I took Margarita to do the laundry, I went to the garden to cut fresh leaves to make my morning tea. I had many herbs and plants to pick from. First, I checked the mint plant, but I passed it. Then, I moved to the oregano pot; I was tempted to take it, but I didn't choose it. Finally, I walked to the ginger root; my mouth watered and I wanted to taste it so badly, but next to it was the rosemary bush with its distinctive, strong smell. The fragrance made me thirsty, and my mouth salivated.

I remembered when I lived in India, my friends made tasty hot drinks from fresh leaves, roots, and dried flowers, Every day they brought me different fresh organic leaves and roots to choose for the three months that I lived and worked in Bombay.

Also, I had worked in Germany, and I used to make pots of tea to drink periodically during the day. In my short stay in China, I tried some exotic Chinese herbal teas, from dried roots, flowers, and seeds. So, I was an expert when I had to make my choice to pick the best fresh garden-grown teas. Usually, I cut and picked different leaves every morning, because I had a lot of knowledge in the selection process.

I don't know what really happened to me when I saw the rosemary bush; it was like it was meant to be… or it was the Devil's trap. I had already made my mind up to go for the ginger root. I had to take only one; there was no room for both of them. I stood for a long time, staring back and forth between the ginger plant, and the rosemary bush.

I forced my brain so hard to make the decision. I remembered my good friend Knus who had inspired me to narrate my own adventure. How I wished to ask him for advice. Certainly, my joy had turned into misery.

I heard a loud voice yelling from the distance, I turned around to see who was calling me.

Anna stood waving at me. "Daddy, hurry up, Mom needs you now", she said. She urged me to come at once. I cut a few branches from the rosemary bush and rushed inside. That was the end of my tea choice. I rinsed the branches for a minute with warm water to make sure all the dust and bugs were washed away. I put them in a pot and filled it up with water. Margarita was staring at me with angry eyes.

Anna asked, "Are you ready, Dad?" I turned the burner on to a high flame. I boiled it for about seven minutes, and I turned it off. Margarita had left to the car. Anna waited next to me, urging me to go. I exited the house and got into the car. I couldn't take my tea because it was hot, and Margarita didn't want to wait longer. I knew that I would be back soon to drink it, so I left the pot cooling and got the car on the road. Ten minutes later, we were helping Margarita to put the dirty clothes in the washing machines. Anna and I went back home because she had to put in her four hours of mandatory school. She was being homeschooled for the third consecutive year, and she loved it. Jokingly, sometimes Margarita and I threatened her that we were going to take her back to regular school. Every time we suggested we were cancelling homeschool, she locked herself up in her room, and cried all day until we agreed to keep her in homeschool. Although, she had to keep getting straight As to be off the hook. I also reminded her that I was her teacher, and I was a tough grader. Indeed, I was happy with her school grades and activities because she was outstanding in every subject but math. I understood her struggle, because I sucked during my elementary and high school years, and I failed all math-related subjects in college.

On the way home, she started a conversation about Margarita, which was related to school and the issue of education. I must add that Anna wasn't my biological daughter, and it bothered her a lot. She asked me a question about it. "Would you stop loving me the way you do now, if you and Mom have a biological child?" I promised her that I wouldn't; that my love for her wasn't going to change for all the wealth on . She added, "What about my brothers? They hate you so much, even though you're the best dad in the whole wide world. Truly, for me and for them you're the best dad ever." She paused for a second, "Let me ask you this, if they said they would live with you on condition that you left me, would you choose them?"

I replied so quickly I almost interrupted her. "I would choose you and not them, of that I am sure." I ended off saying, "Snd God is my witness, I swear it, sweetie."

She didn't stop telling me about her fear of losing me. Anna continued, "Recently, I read on my brother Mario's Instagram 'Anna is not the daughter of Mario Revolori-Quinones, who is the biological father of Mario Jr., Anthony, and Benjamin. She's just his stepdaughter.'"

It made me sad to hear her anguish because I had no idea that my own son had written that awful message on his social media posts. I was speechless. I expected suffering, but not that bad for my dear daughter. God gave me wisdom to speak with authority to protect her. I began slowly, "I love my sons so much, but I love you the same. I forgive them for what they have done to you, and you should forgive them too."

I also mentioned her that I would ask them to forgive me for my mistakes if I had the chance to talk to them. I said, "I'm sure God will reward us. We just have to live one day at the time. I care about you, darling, because you're my daughter and my family. They're my sons, but they aren't part of my family." I told her, there's a huge difference between family members and relatives. A family member can be a blood-related one, or any person who lives in your household and spends his or her time with you. A family member shares food, a house, education, and all extra activities together. A family member also solves his or her differences as one. "You are with me all the time. Your brothers are not going to care for me when I'm in trouble. If I'm hungry, you'll feed me, sick you'll take care of me, when I'm thirsty, you'll bring me a drink, in the hospital you'll visit me. You'll cry for me when I'm in distress. In good times you'll celebrate and laugh with me. They won't do that for me. Let's just pray for them. Remember, Jesus taught us to love even our enemies, and to forgive them."

I asked her the following question, "Tell me sweetie, why was mommy upset this morning?"

She promptly replied, "Well, Mom really misses her teaching job. She doesn't tell you because she's afraid you are not going to listen to her. She needs help. Over there, she had a maid who cooked, and did all the chores for her. Here, she's not happy at work, she's unhappy in our apartment, and she complains about her friends. She told me the other day that all her friends care only about money, cars, drugs, and sex. She wants friends who are producers not consumers, winners not losers. Mom longs for well-educated people around her. People who care about their souls, and their spirits, not just material stuff."

Back at the coin laundromat Margarita had a talk with Sonia, the manager. She said, "I was happy working in El Salvador, you know, I was teaching ninth grade."

Sonia said, "Margarita you never told me what subject you taught."

"Oh, my God, it just slipped my mind," Margarita said, smiling. "I taught Biology. I feel miserable working at that hotel. I don't like the people I work with. They are clowns driving fancy cars; they don't have big dreams. I want to be around successful people, the ones who educate themselves to make a difference in society. But the only one I know who has big dreams is my husband. He already helped his son, Tony Revolori, to become a rich and famous actor. Tony Revolori is best known for the role of Zero in the Oscar award-winning movie "The Grand Budapest Hotel," directed by Wes Andersen, and Flash Thomson in "Spider-Man Homecoming." My husband was his private acting coach, voice coach, agent, manager, and publicist. He invested a fortune in his acting career. In fact, he never could have made it without his dad's support. But Tony stabbed him in the back when he became famous. I fear his two older sons, and his ex- wife might hurt him. He's been receiving death threats from Stuart Stone, a famous casting director in Hollywood. He told Mario to talk to his sons and beg them for forgiveness. His famous son hates him so much that he sent him a nasty email in May 2014. He doesn't know that I read it. But since that day, I've been worried that they could harm him. Mario is the sweetest man, and an awesome dad. I have never seen a father who cares about his sons and daughter like he does. When God created his heart, he poured the gift of fatherhood 110%. He loves, cares, and protects our daughter better than I do. And he did the same when his sons were under his care. His son wrote a message saying he only respects him because he's his father, otherwise he would beat him."

Meanwhile, Anna and I got back home, and I grabbed the pot to pour some tea in my cup. I was surprised when I lifted the lid and saw brown oily foam and pieces of spoiled fish oil and scales. Two weeks later I found out an Indian assassin had poured Dart Frog's skin in it.

The tea was nasty, and I showed it to Anna who was next to me. She leaned over to take a look, and said, "Yucky!" then told me to throw it away. For some unknown reason, I didn't listen to her. I cleaned the rotten stuff from it, using my hand as a strainer. I poured myself a cup and drank it in three minutes. I don't know what I was thinking because as soon as I finished the first cup, I poured a second one. I felt out of control; all I wanted to do was drink as many cups as I could. By the time I drank the third, and final one, I came back to my senses. By then, it was too late. I felt a sharp pain in my lower back. My neck dropped to my chest, vertigo, and unbalance overwhelmed me, and my brain gave me three warning clicks. I felt miserable, I had no physical strength, and my spirit was failing. I remember yelling to Anna, telling her I'd been poisoned. Of course, I was thinking about the Stuart Stone threats. Anna came to help me. In three minutes, my stamina, and energy came back, and I managed to stand. I moved the chair to the computer and checked it for new emails. I didn't find any. I had been sure that Stuart Stone and his people wanted to kill me, and now I had proof. There was no doubt that he had poured some kind of venom into the teapot.

I left the house, and told Anna, "I'm, done sweetie, I'm going to die for sure." I just knew somebody had come in and put toxins in my drink. I took a long breath to get oxygen to my brain. I warned Anna, "If something bad happens to me, please tell Margarita to go to the police and make a report. She must tell them that Stuart Stone has tried to kill me."

At Sonia's place, Margarita and Sonia were still engaged in a long, happy chat. Sonia is a beautiful, blonde, blue-eyed woman, and one of the girls who used to flirt with me. One time, she even asked me to go out with her.

One morning I went to do the laundry by myself, and she introduced me to her husband. When he went to the restroom, she hugged me, and massaged my hands. Anna told me that she was sure Sonia was in love with me. Margarita trusted Sonia however, and continued telling her stories about me, saying, "My husband is a unique guy. He gets up three to five times a night to pray. He's the most spiritual man I've ever known. He reads the Bible at least three times a day. He teaches Anna the love of God, and he's all about forgiveness. He gets angry like all of us when others hurt him, but he falls on his knees, prays, and forgives quickly and easy. He doesn't attend any church. But he says that the love of Jesus exists everywhere. He attends Mass at the Catholic Church if somebody asks him to go. He also goes to Evangelical services when he's friends invite him. He loves to go into the forests to meditate and pray. I have even seen him praying in restrooms when he has to."

Sonia cut Margarita off for a moment. "That's why he doesn't listen to me, she said with a big phony smile.

Margarita asked her, "What do you mean, Sonia?"

She faked the answer, "Well, I asked him if he likes to drink alcoholic beverages, and he did not answer me. A week ago, I asked him about drugs. But he did not want to talk about it. When I brought up the subject that the government should legalize marijuana, he just looked down. Your husband is a good man, Margarita. You should take good care of him, otherwise another woman will charm his heart, and take him away from you," Sonia warned.

Margarita and Sonia were having a good time tittle-tattling. I went to collect Margarita, but she wasn't ready. Anna went inside to call her while I stayed in the car, in agony, waiting for them. Sonia waved me good-bye. On the way home, I told Margarita that I didn't feel good.

Anna interrupted me, "Dad got poisoned. We believe Stuart Stone did it. He put snake venom in his pot of tea. Dad removed the toxin and drank three cups. Maybe he drank five cups." Margarita became worried and wanted me to go to the doctor. I refused, and said that I was going to be fine.

The day went by extremely slowly for me. My spirit and flesh were failing little by little. I reassured myself that I wasn't alone, Jesus stood by my side. He whispered to me, "Yes, I will be with you till the end." He repeated close to my ear the words, "Pray, pray, and pray, unless you fall into temptation." He gave me strength when I thought about surrendering my life to the pain that I was going through. I counted the hours, the minutes, and even the seconds that were staying in the past. I wanted to go back in time, but it was gone. I had drunk the tea, even though I saw the contamination in it. I had cleaned it with my own hands and seen it with my own eyes. I didn't use any logic. Nonetheless, I didn't give up to my praying. I kept asking God to wash away my sins, and to take care of my daughter and my wife. The day had almost ended. I could see the sunbeams filtering in the clouds and hiding forever from my eyes. In my mind this was going to be the last day I'd be with my precious wife, and my beautiful daughter.

Centinella Hospital

I was in pain the whole time, but I made it through the night alive. That night was a long and painful wait, but I kept praying the whole time. I rolled over and twisted on the bed without getting any sleep. I got weaker and weaker every minute. Margarita tried to stay awake with me. Eventually, she couldn't keep up, and fell asleep. I wanted to run, yell, and talk to get rid of the fatigue. Sadly, my brain and my body did not listen to me anymore. At four in the morning, I got up and moved to the living room and dragged myself to the couch. I went through hell for the next three hours. At about seven in the morning, I tried to get up, but my left hand was numbed, and my right leg got weak. I pushed myself up several times, but my body had just given up. I became really afraid and called Margarita. She rushed out from the bedroom and came to assist me. Anna heard the voices and stepped out to help me too.

Margarita massaged my weak leg and asked Anna to pull and stretch my left arm. I moaned in pain; the time of my healthy body and mind was gone. Stuart Stone had me in checkmate. All I could do was pray and wait to die. I asked Margarita, "Who *is* Stuart Stone really?" Then I said to her, "Why is he doing this to me?"

Margarita shrugged and told me, "Don't worry, everything is going to be fine."

"Yes, darling," I said, "but he persecutes me when I haven't done anything wrong to him, or anybody else that I'm aware of." I thought back to some months before, when I read a special email from the real Stuart Stone, and he asked, "Mario, who are you going to vote for?"

I answered him, without thinking, "Donald Trump."

He replied, "Mario, you're awesome. I will vote for Trump too." He added, "I'm asking you because you're a Hispanic and they get mad if you support Trump, but you are a good citizen, I know now." After Donald Trump announced that he was going to run for President of the United States of America, I prayed five to ten times a day for blessings to America and to protect him. Jesus gave me visions, revelations, and prophesies that Donald Trump had been chosen to become President, and he would win because he was the anointed one. The Lord even told me that he was the King David of modern times, and he was going to keep protecting and blessing him, but he was going to be attacked and hated. The Lord also told me he was going to fight for him as he did for King David and no one would touch him. Jesus told me that he had been chosen to clean the swamp. Because I already knew that he was going to win the 2016 election, I had told Margarita and Anna about it. I also shared with them that I was going to vote for the first time in my life.

My relatives, close friends, and clients hated me, and called me racist because I told them I would vote for Donald Trump whenever they asked me who I was going to vote for. I assured them he was going to win because God had already told me. They laughed and said that I was crazy and a traitor because the majority of Hispanics had been brainwashed for generations and voted Democrat. Jesus gave me revelations that he was with Donald Trump, and there is no way he was going to let him lose the election. I'm neither Republican nor Democrat, but I was following the Lord's revelations about Trump.

My mind brought me back to present time, and I looked at Anna and Margarita. "I've got it!" I yelled. "Jesus teaches us in Matthew 5, 11: 'Blessed are you when they insult you and persecute you and utter every kind of evil against you (falsely) because of me. Rejoice and be glad, for your reward will be great in heaven. Thus, they persecuted the prophets who were before you.'"

Yes! My two sons hated me. My brother Henry accused me falsely, my own mother never called me to say hello. My brothers and sisters wouldn't visit me because they were jealous and envious of me. In three days, I would know that my sons even had spoken with the fake Stuart Stone before and after I got poisoned. I thought and said that maybe they hatched this plot together. Yes, I thought all of these horrible things.

"You know something," I told Margarita, "I love my sons and Stuart Stone. I forgive them all, and I ask them to forgive me. May the Lord bless them; even if they are the ones who set traps and all kind of snares to nail me to the cross." That moment, I felt that I was speaking from the innermost part of my heart. I didn't have any evidence to back up that Stuart Stone or anyone else had put poison in my drink. Stuart Stone was just a suspect, and only time was going to give me a true answer.

I added in a soft and weak voice a last bit of advice for Margarita and Anna. "You girls listen to me, and you'd better keep me in your heart. Even though I haven't joined any church, if I die, you should find help in any good Christian church. This is my take on it: I love all churches because they provide help to heal the spirit. All of them have faults, but men have founded them with one purpose, and that's to praise the Lord. I heard a lady speaking her mind the other day while I was walking through an ally in a dirty apartment building. She claimed that we must go to church to serve God well and be perfect or not walk in His path at all. I meditated about that phrase all day, and I came to the conclusion that she was deadly wrong. I know that the Holy Spirit opened my mind, and I came up with an answer. I concluded that no one—absolutely nobody—follows Jesus perfectly. We are all sinners; we cannot, and will not keep God's commandments one hundred percent; we all break them all the time. But we must do our best to praise His holy name, serve him, honor him, and obey his commandments. He will do the rest by taking away our sins and giving us everlasting life in the kingdom of heaven. Blessed be his Holy Name. In short, joining a church is better than not going to any church. Honey, seek first the glory and the grace of the Lord, and anything else the Lord will lay on the table for you if you believe and trust in his mercy."

I regained some energy, and Margarita and Anna took me around the block for a few minutes' walk. Suddenly, I lost my balance, and I went down. Luckily, Margarita was on my left side to catch me. Anna walked on my right side, crying. It took us twenty- three minutes to make it back home. Fortunately, I got there in the nick of time. Anna opened the door for me. I put one foot in, and while I was bringing the other one inside, I collapsed. Margarita caught me as my body was about to hit the tile. Anna grabbed me to lower me very gently and slowly to the floor. Margarita began to cry and panic. Anna called our acquaintances in the front house, for we were living in the guesthouse in the backyard. Margarita phoned her friend, Renee. They all came within three minutes.

"I'll call the paramedics," Renee said. All this happened on the morning of December 18, 2016 at exactly 8:09 in Inglewood, California. I could hear the big aircraft engines roar as they approached for landing in the Los Angeles International Airport on that foggy morning. The loud sounds of the planes didn't let me hear the ambulance, and fire trucks' sirens as they were coming close to take me to the hospital.

The living room was crowded in a minute. Renee came near Margarita and whispered in her ear. Someone else has already called 911 before her. I knew Stuart Stone's people were watching me on hidden cameras, and they had made the call for the paramedics to take me to a place they had already chosen. I got anxious and worried for Margarita and Anna's safety. I rolled my eyes back to warn Margarita, but she wasn't looking at me. I wanted to tell her verbally, but we had a full house, and I didn't know if I could trust everybody. A couple of minutes later, the paramedics came in. They ordered all the bystanders to leave the room, and only Margarita and I stayed to answer questions. They started to ask me routine questions. I replied to them myself, but when I told them that someone had tried to poison me, they ignored me and directed all their questions at Margarita. Everything seemed weird at this point: An unknown person had notified them that I needed medical help. They refused to jot down my answers. Two female paramedics rolled me onto a stretcher and carried me to the ambulance. Margarita was with me, and the paramedic next to me told her not to listen to me because I was mentally ill.

"Sadly, your husband is going crazy," she said to her. Strangely, they were driving around through small streets to the hospital. Centinella Hospital was less than two miles away from my house. It took them more than half an hour to reach the emergency room.

After a long and agonizing drive around, they checked me in with the emergency room personnel. As usual in hospitals, it took them a long time to register me. They took my vitals, and everything was normal. No fever, no high blood pressure, and a normal pulse. They started the interrogatory process. First, an Afro-American nurse asked me what had happened. When I said that I had been accidentally intoxicated drinking a homemade tea, she paid special attention, and she tried to help me for the rest of her shift. She gave me some hope, but when the doctor came to evaluate me, everything changed for the worst.

My destiny was settled; some bad dudes were pulling the strings to make my life miserable. I didn't panic, I knew the Lord was caring for me, and it was Jesus who was going to bring down my aggressors, whoever might have been working with Stuart Stone. For the rest of the day, they kept me waiting to know if they were going to admit me or not. The night came slowly, but the doctor hadn't notified Margarita. I begged them for a glass of water and a bite to eat because I was starving and thirsty. They just ignored me. I just had to smell the French fries that the patient next to me was eating. I spent the night in the emergency room.

The next morning at 9:33, December 19, I had been in the emergency room for twenty-five hours without any medical treatment, food, or water. At about 10:45, they admitted me, but they said I had to wait until 7:55 in the evening for them to bring me to the room. They hadn't given me food, medicine, or liquids yet, except an injection to lower my blood pressure, which had risen extremely high in the previous three hours.

Admitted

Jagdeep Tung, MD, gave Margarita the good news that I was going to be officially admitted, after more than thirty-four hours of waiting. That good news soon turned into bad news. They didn't have a bed ready for me to bring me to the next available room.

By the time they put me in the room, I was suffocating, I was in agony, I was starving, my mouth was dry, and I was choking to death. I asked for food and drink, but they refused to do the swallowing test. I started to feel very dizzy and dehydrated for the lack of nutrients in my body, and for the reaction to the venom that I had taken more than forty-eight hours before.

Finally, a nurse brought me to the room, and thirty-five minutes after I was in bed, visitors came to see me. I was blessed that they poured as rain falling in the desert to support me. They were my clients and friends whom Margarita had notified the day before. She asked me if I wanted her to find my sons, my mother, my brother, and sisters.

I said, "Please make sure no family member or relatives are aware of my sickness." I added to my answer, "And if I die, please bury me without telling my sons or any relatives about my death." I was jotting down in a notebook my questions and answers to Margarita because I was at a 7 on the Glasgow Coma Scale, and I had already lost my voice. I was completely paralyzed and couldn't move my body an inch or turn my head. But I was able to move and bend my right hand to write.

Two hours passed, and Margarita came to tell me that my two sons were coming to the room. I had a negative reaction to the warning. I got upset, for I thought she had called them. I started to pray in silence to calm myself down. They came to my bed to give me a hug. It was the first time they had visited or talked to me for more than three years. I blessed them in my prayers, and I thanked God for having them sent to my deathbed. I asked Margarita for the pen and the notepad to write a couple of questions to them. I scribbled, "Thank you for coming, bros." I remembered that when they lived with me, I gave them everything I could. Literally, I went every place with them. They called me 'bro' all the time. And they considered me the best dad, the best brother, the best friend, and the greatest spiritual leader ever. They even teased me with their girlfriends, who thought I was their big brother, and they flirted with me.

I told them that I was going to die; I was sure about it. They answered me, "No, bro, you're strong. You're going to make it. You're not dying, not just yet." I felt they were not being honest; my gut feelings were revealing their real thoughts to me. They didn't mean what they were saying. The distance was a mile long between their souls and mine. They just said words without real meaning or feeling. They didn't worry about me either. There was disrespect, a little bit of jealousy, and hate in their words.

For a moment, I had thought they really came to see me with humble hearts. I rejoiced to see that my sons had come to their senses and had forgiven my errors and my mistakes, and that they loved me as a brother, as a friend, and most importantly, as their dad. But they spoke harshly, asking me rude questions. At one point, I asked for the pen and the notepad. I wrote down, "I thank you, bros, for visiting me." I wrote a second line and asked them, "How did you hear that I was in the hospital?"

Tony answered me arrogantly, "Stuart Stone called us and gave us the hospital name and the room number." I had feared this all along, and my son's reply proved that I wasn't wrong. I tried to open my eyes to look them straight in their eyes, but my vision was gone, and I was seeing in colors swirling from blue to red and back again. So, I couldn't see their faces. I continued to pray silently. A few minutes passed, then I asked them to pray with me. I cried inside because it took me back in time to when I used to pray five to ten times a day with them. After we finished our prayer, they excused themselves and said that they had to leave.

"It is all about business pops," Tony told me. I answered them that it was fine with me. They had spent about twenty minutes with me, and then they walked out the door. I begged Tony and Mario to bring my youngest son, Benjamin if they visited me again. I hadn't seen my baby son since he was twenty-two months old, and he was already five. I had forgotten what he looked like.

An hour after my boys left, the room was crowded with relatives. My mother, Nita, was crying and praying for me; most of my brothers and a sister showed up at the same time.

All of my relatives were informed by Stuart Stone's people that I was hospitalized. I had been on the run from him for the past five months. Now he had me cornered, sick, and close to death, but he did not show any mercy and wanted to cut me piece by piece until I was finished and bled no more. Certainly, he wished me dead. I did not know why, though. But I also knew, deep in my soul, that he wasn't going to be successful because Jesus was battling on my behalf against him and his army of demons.

During my first official night at Centinella Hospital, my mother and other family members left one at the time around twelve. In a minute, no one was in my room, except Margarita and Anna. Many of my loyal friends were still in the waiting room. They wanted to visit me in the room, or at least to know how I was doing. A few of them stayed as late as one in the morning. Anna was going to be taken by one of my best friends to sleep over at our friend, Renee's, home. But on that night, she was safe, for the nurse had allowed her to spend the night with me in the hospital room.

I didn't trust anybody. I knew Anna was being followed. I feared Stuart Stone wanted to harm her. No one believed me, but my thoughts never stopped ringing in my head, telling me to find extra protection for her.

Anna's life was in danger, but only in my thoughts because my brain put it in my feelings. But no one cared what I thought.

I asked Margarita to cancel the internet account immediately, and to change our cell phones. I warned her that someone was inside the hospital working for Stuart Stone, who wouldn't stop punishing me.

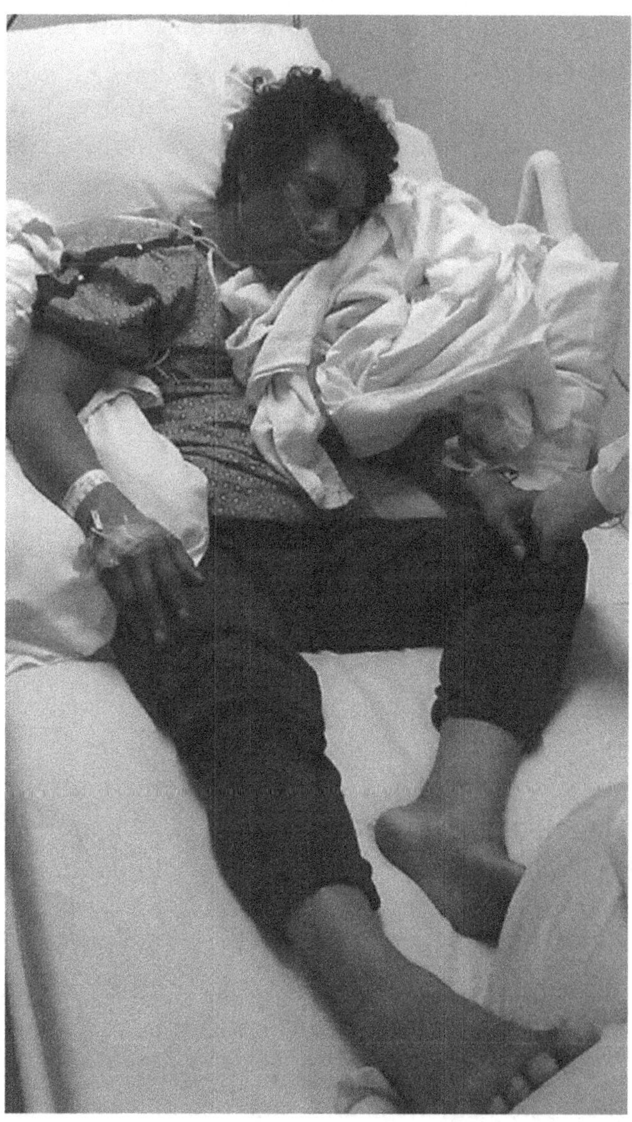

Centinella Hospital (December 18, 2016–January 7, 2017)

Stroke

After all the visitors had left, Margarita and Anna went to catch some sleep in the chairs next to my bed. It was already three in the morning. I was sad for what Margarita and Anna were going through; they didn't have blankets to cover them, and they were slumped on the chairs. I called them every ten minutes to come and turn my head. It had been a tough day for them. They became my personal angels, sent by Jesus to take care of me.

A new day came. The first thing I asked Margarita was to get me some food and water. It was about seven in the morning, December 20. She did everything she could to feed me. She went to talk to the nurse to ask her for food and water. The nurse said that Dr. Nazari, the neurologist in charge, needed to evaluate me first. I agreed, but the problem was that Dr. Nazari never came the whole day. Another day went by for me without food or liquids in my stomach. Margarita called her boss and took the whole week off to be with me at the hospital.

The night shift nurse came to check my vitals. I wrote a note to her to pass to Dr. Nazari that I had been poisoned and the suspect was Stuart Stone and his men. She just laughed at me, then turned around and left the room without saying a word. It was clear that all hospital personnel had made their minds up and were not going to treat me or feed me yet. I just went back to what I have done best since childhood. I engaged my heart, my mind, my brain, my soul, my whole body, and my mouth to talk to the Lord. I got deep in my prayers, and "I AM WHO I AM" came to visit me from heaven; not in a burning bush like he showed up to Moses more than three thousand years ago, but in a vision to strengthen my heart, to renew my spirit, and to give me strength. Certainly, the Lord was going to be with me healing and rescuing me every step of the way. At that moment, more than a hundred people fell on their knees in five countries to join me in prayer for healing and forgiveness. Jesus is the way, the truth, and the life.

I was determined to prove to doctors, friends, and relatives that all the hospital personnel were plotting evil against me. Since Stuart Stone had given me poison in a hot cup of tea, I was determined to show Margarita that they were not going to rest in their efforts to harm Anna and me. She did not believe that I was telling the truth either. I cleared my thoughts with constant prayers, so I wouldn't think I was going crazy, as the doctors, nurses, my sons, my mother, and brothers made even Margarita believe.

Another day passed with my stomach empty and me starving to death. I was practically passing out from starvation. I felt sever dizziness, and my body needed fluids soon. I pleaded for food and drink, but they gave me nothing. Dr. Nazzari was still a no-show while I was dying. My breathing was failing fast. Finally, a nurse ordered oxygen for me. The oxygen didn't help a bit, so they rushed me to the intensive care unit. I spent the first night of my entire life with oxygen around the clock.

The new day brought sunrays through the windows. I knew it was another day, and I tried to keep track, but I had already lost the count. I must have repeated in my head a hundred times: "Is today December 23, 24, 25, or 26? I wasn't sure about the day or the date. Christmas was around the corner, in my mind. Sadly, I couldn't keep count of the days from the December 22. I was too sick, weak, and starving to death to remember. I began to forget names and days, but I was alert, praying at all times, and the praying kept me going and alive.

I wrote to the nurses about three to five times a day, asking to run a test for poisoning. I hadn't seen the doctor since the day I saw the emergency doctor who had admitted me.

I waited in hell for a very long time to see the doctor. Finally, one afternoon, Dr. Nazzari came in for the first time, and saw me for merely a minute. I tried to write a note to tell him about the poison that I had drunk, but he refused to read it. Instead, he ordered me to speak out. In my mind, I asked him to run a poisoning test. I thought he heard me because he turned his head and gave me a diabolical laugh. As he was leaving, he yelled, "You had a stroke it wasn't that massive, so stop whining. A CAT scan, and MRI tests are going to be done tomorrow."

I did not know that it was December 26, 2016 already. I didn't want to ask, but I heard my evil brother, Henry, who had come in to stay with me, asking Margarita how she had spent her Christmas. They were talking about the food and gifts. She was taking a nap because she was tired and sleepy.

She said, "I've been here since Christmas, and today is already the 26th. I spent the whole of Christmas Day in this room. In fact, I haven't gone back home since then." The joy of the Christmas celebration was over, and I was not aware of it. But I was still alive and fighting for my life. Margarita had been in the hospital room with me twenty-four hours a day for the past eight days, making sure I received everything I needed. I wished the doctors would listen to me and run a test to cure my poisoned body. But I started to give up hope. I knew if they didn't feed me within a day or two, I was going to die.

The morning of December 27, they took me to the CAT scan exam. An hour later, they got me in the MRI cylinder to run the test. About seven hours later, the results came in. It wasn't a surprise to me that both of them were negative. Dr. Nazzari was just wasting time, and it was my precious time. I even told Margarita that he was stubborn as a mule. I just knew better than any doctor in the world what was wrong with me. I had swigged the tea I had been threatened with by Stuart Stone. But the time had not come for Jesus to show his mighty hand for a miraculous healing yet.

The nurse came to inform Margarita that the test results were in and that the results were normal. She said that my brain looked better than ever. I had been telling them all along what had caused the damage to my body and mind. She also mentioned that Dr. Nazzari was going to come to talk to me in about two hours. It was about three in the afternoon. I waited those two long hours to see the doctor.

I could not take a single breath on my own. Margarita had to lift my right hand for me to catch a little air. It looked funny, but that was the mechanism my brain used to breathe. I was choking every minute from lack of oxygen. They had the oxygen on me, but it suffocated me as well, so I was in a dilemma. It was a matter of surviving by faith in miracles. My body didn't respond to any kind of medicine. That same night, at seven o'clock, my two older sons visited me for the second and last time at the hospital. As I had asked, they brought my youngest son, Benjamin Matthew Revolori. Oh! How much I wished to hug him and to tell him that I'd missed him, and that I loved him a lot. But I was paralyzed, blind, and mute, so I couldn't tell him anything.

I prayed for him in silence, for that's all I could do. My two older sons were putting trash in Margarita's head. They didn't know I was listening to them. They told her that I wasn't ill, that I was faking the whole thing, and that I was an evil father. They advised her to separate from me because I was playing mind games with her. They warned her that I had made up the Stuart Stone story. They said I had sent the threats to myself and that I had emailed them to my own email address using the fake name of Stuart Stone. Tony even asked her to let them delete the email threats from my computer and cell phone. When I heard them, my heart wept a river. I grew sad and depressed, and I wished to die at that instant. They came to visit me for about thirty minutes and left.

On December 30, at eight in the morning, a Mexican guy in a straw hat, and not in hospital uniform, took me to the operating room. The nurse told me that the doctor finally had scheduled a lumbar puncture to be done to remove the poison from my lower back. This was the treatment I'd been asking for all along, to suck out all the poison stored on my back. The guy who pushed the bed left me outside the door in the long and dark hallway for as long as forty-five minutes, unattended. Then a large African-American man opened the door. He saw me and gave me a hateful look. He went back inside and closed the door behind him.

Some minutes later, the same man opened the door. This time he brought me inside the operating room. They turned me on my back and punctured my skin. There were two doctors working on my back.

One of them said to the other, "I have never seen so much venom in a patient. I hope we are able to suction it all out." I predicted it was going to be a miracle for them, but I knew the Lord is awesome and they would get it all out.

The other doctor responded, "They waited too long to bring him here."

That same day at noon, they installed a nose feeding tube. They tried to feed me for the first time in twelve days. Things got worse. I became allergic, and my nose swollen up. They had to remove it within minutes. I kept fighting against all odds, but what worried me the most was that I knew that Stuart Stone was going to try to kill me inside the hospital, and that he was following Anna everywhere she went.

A few days before, my brother Tony, his wife, and their four-year-old son had come to visit me from Silver Spring, Maryland. Margarita let him drive my Honda, which I thought was a big mistake, but I didn't tell her that he was going to get us in trouble with the car. Actually, I was wrong because many months later, I was going to find out that my brother saved my life and Anna's.

After the lumbar puncture, all my friends joined me to pray for a miracle. I begged my friends and relatives to intercede for me for forgiveness, and healing, and protection for Margarita and Anna, to take care of and support them. I requested, one last time, for to the doctor to feed me through my mouth. However, he refused to do the swallowing exam to find out if they could do so.

I was sure that Jesus was with me all the time. I asked Jesus not to take away my mind or my voice, because deep in my heart I wanted to glorify Him till the last second of my life. I began to get ready to die, and I was asking the Lord for forgiveness, even for Stuart Stone, and to care for my two girls when I went to heaven. I sure I was going to be gone soon. My life had ended, as far as I was concerned. January 2, 2017, Dr. Nazzari made up his mind to feed me, and scheduled an endoscopic surgery for the placement of a gastrostomy tube to feed me with it. I didn't have difficulty to swallowing food or liquids, but they refused to evaluate me on the swallowing issues.

Knus had warned me about this deadly pseudo-stroke long before. However, he never mentioned to me that it was going to be an almost perfect crime, orchestrated by a professional assassin and my own relatives.

After that day, I started to have a little hope of surviving. The nurse fed me for the first time in almost two weeks. I felt like a magic potion had entered my bloodstream when the liquid from fruits and vegetables reached my stomach. They fed me three times a day until January 7, 2017, when I was kicked out of bed, and they left me unattended in the hallway for more than nine hours, waiting to be picked up by my friends and my wife.

Finally, Jesus was feeding – the Lord changed Dr. Nazzari's heart to have a little compassion for me. So, I tasted my first meal on January 2, 2017, at about eight in the evening. I went to rest that night for the first time in many sleepless nights because my stomach was full, and my brain had enough nutrients to start waking up.

The Arrest

My mind took me a few days back. The sun rose on December 28, 2016. My body was getting weak because it needed a good serving of food and liquids. I wanted to yell to the nurse to get her attention, to ask her to give me some vegetables and fruits. Henry was saying that he was going to eat a banana, and I wanted so badly to take a bite out of it.

As I said earlier, Tony supposedly came to take care of me. He and his wife, Lilly, only came to visit me a couple of times. The truth? He came to take a long vacation. He was cruising around driving the Honda, and the two times he came to see me, he had driven it to the hospital. I argued a little with Margarita because she let him use our car and go wherever he pleased. My other brothers also drove it. I wanted to know the reason all of them drove it, and parked their own vehicles. All these questions were stuck in my brain, but Jesus was going to answer them in time. My brothers and my sons meant to hurt me, but the Lord turned it into rewards for me.

Tony was cruising around the LAX area one night. It was December 24, and someone rear-ended him on purpose. He was working for Stuart Stone, which I found out three months later in March 2017 when Farmer's Insurance contacted me. They told me that they were not going to pay to repair it, because the driver who hit it didn't have a current policy with them at the time the accident had occurred back on December 24, 2016. At the scene of the accident, the driver came to Tony and begged him not to call the police because he was in a hurry. Tony believed him, and they just exchanged drivers' licenses and insurance policy cards.

Clearly, Stuart Stone had his men following the Honda twenty-four hours a day. They wanted to find Anna. I just knew that Stuart Stone wanted to harm her. But I didn't know the motive and how he was planning to do it.

Thanks to Tony, my two sons, and other family members who were wrecking my brand-new Honda CR-V, I was going to prove to them that Stuart Stone had me on his wanted list, and he was getting ready to kidnap and hurt my sweet, innocent daughter. He thought he had me on the radar, and it was only a matter of time to find Anna and pick her up. He wasn't counting on the fact that I had an army of angels on my side, and the Commander-in-Chief was Jesus Christ.

Stuart Stone got busy tracking the Honda to get to Anna. Every time the van was driven, he and his men followed it. They started on December 19, when Henry drove it out of the driveway for the first time. Stuart Stone didn't have an idea that Anna had been hiding in the neighbors' house the whole time. That intense tracking went on for eight days. Margarita and my relatives said that I had lost my mind every time I told them to watch out for Anna, because Stuart Stone wanted me dead, but he needed to find and kidnap Anna first, then kill me. They told me it was only my imagination. Obviously, Henry and my two sons didn't say a word because they knew I was telling the truth, and they were deleting the emails and the text threats Stuart Stone had sent me. They just looked at each other and pretended to listen to me. They had been attacking me since the first day they came to visit me at the hospital. The FBI report showed that Stuart Stone made a successful tracking activity on Tuesday, December 20, at 2:14 in the morning. He was tracking the Honda CR-V driven by Tony. The next time was December 25, right on Christmas Day. Both tracking activities happened in the city of Inglewood a few blocks from Centinella Hospital.

Stuart Stone was gambling big, and he wasn't expecting that Jesus was giving him a few more days of freedom. He had planned to cut me to pieces, but in the end, he was going to get caught in his own trap. Meanwhile, back in the intensive care unit, I continued praying for deliverance, forgiveness, and blessings for all my friends, my foes, my relatives, and especially, for Anna, Margarita, and myself. Margarita was almost fainting and never moved away from my side, holding my hand the whole time. Margarita's sacrifice was my Christmas present for that bitter December 24 and 25, 2016.

But on the streets, my brother, his wife, and other relatives including my mother were having the time of their lives, beating up the Honda CR-V, and celebrating the holidays.

On December 28, 2016, I was in critical condition. I was giving up hope, but my wife never surrendered; she encouraged me every second to take a deep breath. I listened to her and together, holding hands, the hours passed by. I pictured myself at the edge of a cliff ready to jump off to end my life. I wanted to finish the race to stop my mental suffering and to end my physical pain. Certainly, in my life I had made mistakes, I had committed sins, but I had loved the Lord and I worked hard to strengthen my spirit every day of my life. I asked the Lord to reward me for all the good I had done and forgive my sins. I kept these questions in my mind: "Am I going to enter the kingdom of God Almighty? Did I do well enough for my soul to be chosen?"

Margarita told me that for the previous five months she had been getting visions. At least she thought they were revelations from the Lord. She had told me many times that something big and good was going to happen to us in the future. She thought it was going to come true one day at 11:11 in the morning. She had been beholding strange events when the time was 11:11 at work and at home. She also mentioned that many emails from Stuart Stone came at 5:11, 8:11, 10:11, whether day or night. She saw the visions only when the last four digits ended in ones. I believed her story and kept it in mind, and every time I received a message from Stuart Stone that ended in double-one patterns, it gave me the chills, and I became nervous. The December 28 was gone, and a new day came. And it was already the 29th.

Margarita went home at nine that morning of December 28th, and she had left me with Henry, who took care of me that morning, and the night of the 28th. She went home to catch some sleep and to take care of

Anna. She came back at about nine in the morning the next day, which was the 29th. She was excited but irritated at the same time. She looked angry, and she wanted to tell me something important. I could hear, but I couldn't talk back or see yet. I was getting weaker every minute.

I asked to her to tell me whatever she had in mind. I didn't expect she was going to give me a million-dollar piece of news. I waited patiently for her to start. She took a deep breath and cleared her throat.

In tears, she said, "Yesterday, the FBI authorities put Stuart Stone behind bars." I wanted to cheer when I heard this shocking piece of news. She hesitated for a second. "Here's the catch," she continued, "he wasn't Stuart Stone. He was a criminal who was hacking and tracking you while impersonating Stuart Stone. You were right, honey, he was following you, and he was the one who put poison in your drink. Now he's been arrested, and you don't have to fear anymore."

Immediately, I wanted to tell her that she was wrong because he had been the killer, but the criminal minds who had planned the assassination were others. And they were still on the loose, and perhaps inside the hospital or even in my own room. I wanted to tell her I was sure that it was Henry. Nonetheless, I learned for the first time that the killer wasn't Stuart Stone, but an Indian citizen who had hacked me. He also hacked the real Stuart Stone's casting computer. But with my help, the Los Angeles FBI agency had tracked and arrested Hajiv Alair Mhulay Zhamgar when he was trying to pass the hospital door to enter my room. Obviously, he wanted to grind me to dust. I was happy to know that the real talent agent, Stuart Stone who had helped me with Anna's music dreams, was not involved.

I put the puzzle pieces together. When Tony got rear-ended, Hagiv Mhulay's people were following him to find Anna, who was his final target to finish the job. He did not know that Jesus was listening to my prayers. And he was saving me, healing me, and protecting me from all my enemies. I was rejoicing, praying, and singing to God in my hospital bed. The first thing that came to my mind was forgiveness for this poor lost soul. At the same time, I heard Margarita cursing him for what he had done to me. I switched my prayer to ask the Lord for her so she could soften her heart and learn to forgive even Hagiv Mhulay.

Even though Hagiv Mhulay had been locked up, he had people working for him inside the hospital. My brother, Henry, was his main contact, and his men tried to kill me two more times.

The last one happened the day Dr. Nazzasri, an immigrant from the Middle East, scheduled my last surgery to attach the feeding tube to my stomach. An Indian anesthesiologist was hired by Hagiv Mhulay to put me to sleep for good. I heard two Hispanic nurses talking about the anesthesiologist hired to finish the job Hagiv Mhulay had started. Mysteriously, I recovered my voice and my eyesight for a few minutes when the man came to the operating room. He stared at me with an awful murderous look. One of the nurses looked at me with sadness in her eyes. Magically, a higher-ranking doctor showed up and called out the Indian doctor. Finally, an Asian physician walked in and put the feeding tube in place. The same nurse looked at me again, this time with joy, and a big smile. She told me, "You're safe."

I replied, "Yes, it's the miracle I've been praying for, and Jesus heard me." Four hours later, I woke up with a hose hanging down from my navel, unable to see or talk.

The Hand

Once again, I'm going back to one of the earlier days, when I was waiting to die in the hospital. I couldn't keep track of the days, but Margarita kept me posted with the new events. On this particular night I asked her, and she told me it was the December 30, 2016, two days after Hajiv Mhulay was caught and arrested, and the time was around nine in the evening. I reminisced about the time that I spent with my father, from when I was about five years old, until July 2012 when he took his last breath.

I cried tears of blood through my heart, and my sorrow grew. I remembered what a gentleman he was. Indeed, he was one of the best dads in the whole world. He always supported me, educated me, and he went the extra mile with me when I needed him the most. He faced danger to save me. On the other hand, he was the toughest father I had ever met and known. He was strict and didn't let me get away with bad behavior without punishment. I remember one time, Michael Angel, a rich ranch-owner's kid, gave me a wooden toy. The boy's dad found out and told my father that I had stolen the toy from his son. My dad punished me for the whole day, and he went with me to apologize to Michael Angel and his father. Years later, I reminded him that he had chastised me for something I didn't do. Michael Angel had given me the toy of his own free will. But my dad was awesome; he really cared for me. He taught me to pray and to read the Bible at the age of six. Several times, he and I slept in temporary tents built with tree branches and straw. We did it once a year to take care of the crops in the fields and to keep thieves away from stealing our grains, vegetables, and fruits. Pops and I used to go to sleep between ten and eleven every night. We took turns to lead the prayers before we went to rest. I could see the stars hanging down from the blue sky, and every so often, I spotted shooting stars and asked my dad all kind of questions about them. He always had an answer for all the questions that I asked him. And every time he started saying, "When God created it," and he gave me a physical explanation.

At home, he used to read his Bible every day at dusk, and he sat in a rocking wooden chair. He read it with me on his lap. Dad couldn't read very well for he taught himself how to read and write as an adult in his village. He had tons of friends who loved him, and a handful of guys who hated him for telling the truth about anybody and anything. A couple of bad dudes threatened him with guns, machetes, and knives, but no one touched him because he walked with Jesus all the days of his life. Of course, he made many mistakes as a father and as a man. But he never stopped asking for forgiveness; he always repented. He asked for forgiveness and turned back to praise the Lord. One time, he gave me a note, and he said, "To inherit the kingdom of God is only possible if you trust the Lord and receive Jesus, who is the way, the truth, and the life, and our savior." Then he looked at me and said, "Please don't ever forget it." He continued, "Nita is the sweetest wife, the best mother, the best friend, and she has Jesus in her heart. If she doesn't get saved, what chance do I have to enter God's kingdom?"

All of these thoughts were in my prayers while I was preparing my spirit to leave my physical body. I gripped Margarita's hand and squeezed her fingers a little. I got a few distorted sounds out of my mouth to let her know that I was going to die in a minute. She began to cry and told me not to leave her and Anna alone in this messed up world. I wept for a second with one eye, for the other one was open and did not blink at all to shed a single tear. I called my dad to wait for me as I was sure in a matter of seconds, I would join him in the presence of God to spend eternity with Jesus. My father and I were very close friends on earth. I thought I could ask Jesus to set an eternal cot for me next to Dad's bed. I didn't realize that the nurse was watching my vitals on the monitor.

That night, I knew my life was going to end soon. Margarita was watching me; it was about eleven already.

I told her goodbye, and I knew that God was going to receive me with open arms when I entered into his kingdom. Surely, I was going to fly into the wild blue yonder. Margarita began to weep, and I told her, "Don't cry, my dad is already waiting for me."

As I said, my dad and I always stuck together in life. I had the best dad ever, but I did not have the best mother. I love my mother the same way I loved my dad, but I'm sorry to say there's no comparison between the two of them. I respect and admire her, but my dad taught me to speak the truth even if it is a matter of life and death. My mother called me only once to say hello, and she did it because I once asked her why she called my brothers and sisters every day but she never called me. She phones me a few times when she needed my help to solve her problems. I wasn't the perfect son, but I respected her, I obeyed her, I took good care of her legally and financially, and I always followed the Lord as she wanted me to do. Meanwhile, all my brothers caused her all kinds of problems and my sisters took advantage of her. In my death bed, I was trying to be fair with my mother and my dad. I didn't want to be biased, but I couldn't deny this truth.

I prayed: "Dear God, I love my mom dearly, and I bless her. I especially ask for her health, forgiveness, and for a long happy life. I hope and pray Jesus will bless her. He'll give her the strength to pray for my soul to rest in peace, for I'm the worst sinner of all her twelve children. I hope she'll enjoy the presence and blessings of the Lord for the rest of her life." That was my last request for my dear mom.

After I finished my long prayer, I thought I squeezed Margarita's hand again. At that same moment, I took a special breath, and I heard the nurse watching the monitor saying, "Oh my God, I just saw Mario's aura coming out. That was the most beautiful thing I've ever seen."

I stretched my arms and legs out to surrender my spirit, and the wires disconnected. The monitor turned off, and the nurse—a very honest, kind, and hardworking Filipino guy—came running into my room.

I felt that something unknown from the deepest of my being came out. My heart felt a sublime sensation. My lips curved into a tiny smile, and my mind whispered to the wind that was blowing around me. "I'm coming in a second, please carry me away to heaven." My mind stopped with the conversation I had with myself. I was already out of the real world.

Margarita's yelled to me, "Please, don't leave me. What am I going to do without you?" I wanted to see her face one last time with my human eyes. But my time on earth was over. I just saw the sadness and agony on her face with the eyes of my spirit. At that instant, how I wished to talk to her one last time and tell her how much I loved her, and to ask her to forgive all the mistakes and the troubles I had caused her as a husband, as a man, and as a brother. I wanted to beg her to take good care of Anna for me.

Soon I jumped to the side restricted to mortals and landed on celestial soil. Margarita remained in the past, and I went into the house of God for many seconds, at least five minutes. I heard the laughter of demons all around me clapping and singing diabolic songs. All the demons were cheering, dancing, and firing burning brimstone every time they opened their nasty mouths. They seemed very happy. It was like they were celebrating my soul's arrival. I stayed more than five minutes in God's sacred paradise. I spent that time wisely, looking for my dad. Suddenly, the hand of God appeared from the distance. I saw it stretching out toward me. Jesus laid it on the top of my head. God's holy hand stuck on my soft spot, and He raised me up and put me back where Margarita was crying for me.

Jesus's voice was saying, "You're going back to work, to save some of my children." When I came back, the nurse was standing by my bed. He was struggling to put all the wires together and to turn the medical equipment back on.

With a caring voice, he said, "Mario, promise me you are not going to try to commit suicide again." Danny Knus had used the fake names of

Ben Matt to begin my journey, but he used my true and correct last name to start my adventure, my real story, and my encounter with Jesus from childhood to present time. I remember I had never told him anything about the story of my life. Although I have a feeling that my ex-wife had shared with him what had happened to me in the past. He guessed about my future; I believe it was a revelation from God because he even told me that some family members and relatives have been planning to do evil against me. In fact, the nurse thought that I had pulled the wires on purpose to commit suicide. But Margarita was my witness, it hadn't happened like that. I was still listening to the nurse when Margarita's cell phone rang. It was a long-distance call. Her nephew, Elvert, and his wife, Claudia, were calling from El Salvador.

I heard the whole conversation between Margarita and Claudia because Margarita turned on the speaker for me to listen to it. The chat went like this: "Hey, Margarita, I was praying a couple of minutes ago. Elvert and I were asking the Lord to save and heal Mario. I have to tell you, I'm sure that Jesus showed me a miracle. Mario is forgiven and rescued from hell. I saw a bunch of demons trying to take him to hell. They were dancing and singing because they almost had his soul in the underworld. But at that time, I saw the power and the hand of Jesus diving down from heaven to rescue him. He stretched His right hand out and grabbed Mario's head and brought him back to earth. The Lord wants him to go back to glorify and praise His holy name." And that night, the Lord, with his mighty power, took me back from yonder to , from death to life. Jesus rescued and saved me from Satan.

Ann Angel

An angel showed up on December 23, five days before the killer was arrested and locked up to serve a life sentence in prison. God heard my prayer and soon the Lord sent me an angel. I was surprised because I wasn't expecting help—neither spiritual nor physical care—from angels that soon. My own daughter, Anna, turned into my guardian angel. God chose her to care for me during my hard times at the hospital. Anna was only eleven years old. In a vision, I saw this angel coming down from heaven. She was holding a white handkerchief in her hand. I heard the voice of Jesus telling her to wipe my forehead and to moisten my eyes to clean my tears. He also gave her instructions to stay by my side to chase away any demons who would try to get close to me. From that day, I began to listen to her advice and her warnings, and I changed her name. I started calling her Ann Angel because she was chosen to be an angel sent from heaven. My mind warned me that Jesus chose her to take care of me right away, lest those demons do harm to my mind and take my soul with them. She needed to protect me night and day. The Lord said to her, "It's my will that you take good care of your dad. But I have to school him because he has disobeyed me, and he is going to be in a lot of pain for a while. He has followed me all his life, but he has sinned by setting his mind on material richness and evil thoughts. I'll forgive him, but he'll face physical and mental pain for several months."

A second before the revelation ended, Anna stood next to me and with a paper towel in her hand wiped out my left eye to clean all the dirt and dust that my brain was releasing. She went to the sink to moisten the towel every ten to fifteen minutes to repeat the cleansing of my blind eyes.

She did the cleaning every day. She also placed the palms of her hands on my eye to keep it closed. She made sure my eyes did not get dust in, to avoid an eye infection. She became my guardian angel. She was sad because I couldn't play with her like I used to weeks before. Even though I was very strict with her when dealing with education, respect, and moral issues, she was having fun serving, caring, and praying for me. I felt good to have her with me in the hospital because she was safe there. She started to care for me and did some of the nurse's aide jobs for a few days before Hajiv Mhulay was arrested on December 28. But even after he was incarcerated, I feared for her life and my life because Hajiv wasn't cooperating. According to the FBI, they investigated other unknown trackers following the Honda in several places. He was tracking and hacking me from Frankfurt, Germany, from Chicago, New York, and Los Angeles.

I became very dependent on her care and bonded more to her company. I could not live without her around my bed. One night, she stepped out of the room to go to the cafeteria to get some food and drinks. Margarita and Ann Angel went when I dozed off, and I didn't know that they had left. A minute later I noticed they were gone, I burst out crying, and my eyes ran a river of tears. I couldn't control my anguish, and I remembered my three sons whom I missed a lot. How I hoped God would let me see them playing with me one day. But I was dreaming a dream that would never become a reality. Certainly, it won't come to pass in my lifetime. These were the sad thoughts that came back and forth in my fatigued and ill brain. My sons and I had been brothers and best friends since they were born, except the last three years they went their own way with their mother. I wept and prayed to Jesus to forgive me for I wasn't the father they wanted me to be. I was blaming myself for my mistakes, and for the sins I had committed. I pleaded with the Lord to forgive me and to grant my petitions, and to tell them how much I loved and miss them. Margarita and Ann Angel entered and saw my face soaked in tears. Ann Angel wiped my face slowly and gently. I wrote a note and told her about the anguish and fear. She comforted me and told me that I had been a good father to them. She added that all fathers make mistakes in raising their children. After that, Ann Angel turned into my guardian angel and I had met my Spirit Guide.

She helped me physically and spiritually during the days I spent in that scary hospital room. Ann Angel never left me alone in that dark room. Jesus taught her how to become a nurse, a mother, and a friend to her own dad at an early age. She gave me hope by encouraging me to have faith. Once she told me I was going to make it safe and sound. I asked her to pray for me. She did lead me in prayers day and night. Jesus had sent me Ann Angel to brighten my dark days and to give light to my blind eyes.

Discharged

Dr. Nazzari ordered the nurses to kick me out of the hospital room. My physical therapist complained on my behalf. The speech coach pleaded with him to keep me in bed for at least two more weeks because I was not ready to stand up, sit down, or to go out on my own yet.

A couple of minutes after I got back home in a wheelchair, Jesus gave me spiritual and physical strength. Now I knew I had brought the illness and the suffering upon myself. I could not blame Hajiv Mhulay for poisoning me, or my sons for their errors and for abandoning me. But I had abandoned them, and perhaps I wasn't a good father. One thing I was sure of, I gave them everything I had to raise them in the best way I could, and I had hoped to make them good kids. Although I had disobeyed the Lord by doing what he had told me to stay away from, God spoke to me and brought to my mind wisdom to turn away from sin. I had turned into a lover of material possessions and all kinds of pleasures that burned my spirit and poisoned my flesh. Certainly, my heart had been tossed into the mud because I had committed terrible sins before the eyes of the Lord. I had been following two masters, and Jesus is clear in his teachings. "Do not serve two masters," Jesus says. I needed to stop blaming doctors and the hospital personnel, in order to receive the Lord's healing and blessing. Deep in my heart, I thought that I had sinned, doing wrong things such as the following: I became hooked to fame and fortune; I ran like crazy trying to make a lot of money and I had a lust for sex. A few times, I had watched the wrong videos and movies; I wasn't addicted to it, but I had offended God. I let my mind think about adultery on several occasions. Anger and lies were other issues that I couldn't put away completely. I have never killed anyone, stolen, become drunk, done drugs, or harmed anyone physically or psychologically; because of that I thought I wasn't a big sinner. But I had pushed my sons and daughter to the toughest work habits. Of course, I did it to make them winners. My hope was to save them spiritually, physically, and financially, so they could become better human beings, better citizens, and better sons and daughters. But my discipline and approach to handling pressure was a little harsh for them, not for me. I thought I was doing the right thing, but perhaps I was wrong. Only time will tell me if I was completely right or wrong. I told Margarita that I love my sons and Ann Angel equally, and I'll be waiting for my sons for the rest of my life to come back, so I can give them a true loving hug. My heart longs to hug and kiss them again.

My mind took me back to the hospital. Days were going by slowly for me; I did not see any visible improvement. Dr. Nazzari came to visit me for the last time. I had been hospitalized for Christmas and New Year. Dr. Nazzari was complaining that he did not get paid enough money, and he was threatening to kick me out of the hospital. He mentioned that I didn't have a good insurance. I was covered by an Obamacare policy. He said that my Obama insurance coverage didn't cover his fees nor the payment of the hospital bills to keep me in much longer. That was the last time he showed up to see me. He ordered his nurse to discharge me at once.

On January 7, early in the morning, they moved me out of the room. I waited around eight hours that night for Margarita to arrange transportation to take me home. I was unable to speak, I was blind, and paralyzed. I couldn't sit at all; I needed to be flat on my back. But the nurses put me on a broken wheelchair to wait for my ride for more than eight hours when I was finally taken home. I just had faith and trusted the Lord that I was going to make it through the night. The physical trainer was arguing with the nurse in charge that it was unsafe and inhumane for me to leave the hospital in such critical condition. But it seemed that nothing worked in my favor. I was destined to go home and die in my own bed. Finally, four of my friends came to take me home. They picked up the wheelchair because one wheel was broken, and it didn't roll at all. They brought me down all the way from the upper floor to the parking lot where the car was parked. Somehow, they managed to squeeze me into the Honda van, and they drove me for a five- minute ride from the hospital to my house. They tried to find a place to lie me down because I needed a hospital bed, but I didn't have one. Margarita came up with a great idea to put two sofas together and tied them with ropes to secure them. My future was set to stay in that den for three months, secured in between two couches until we could afford to buy a hospital bed.

Ann Angel Moved Home

The night before I returned home, Ann Angel had been fixing up the place for me. She gave me an awesome welcome. She had posters and notes hanging on the wall for everybody to see. She had been my angel at the hospital, and on my first night back home, she had decided to take care of me as she had done when I was hospitalized. She had been my guardian angel during the time that I was under doctors' care. Now she was my personal nurse, and my second doctor, because my primary doctor was Margarita. Ann Angel had her magic towel in her hands, and she dried my drooling mouth every ten minutes as she used to do at the hospital. She made sure to give me all my natural medicine in time. She put a jar filled with water on a table by my side. She picked a green plastic cup to pour me the water.

From the time, I was discharged from the hospital until May 14, 2017, she got up early in the morning to cook special meals for me. She made chicken soup and three times a day, and squeezed fresh fruit juices. In the afternoons, she fed me all kinds of steamed vegetables and fruit salads. She made sure that I was getting all my omega oils from organic avocado, broccoli, and fish oils. Ann Angel found out that salmon was rich in omega oils, so she began to cook it three times a week. It was the best salmon I'd ever eaten. She always bought the best Pacific wild-caught Alaskan salmon. She marinated it with extra virgin olive oil and added a bunch of fresh oregano herbs picked right from our garden. Dr. Nazzari was completely wrong. I could swallow fine – he just didn't want to feed me. I had been right all the time.

Ann Angel had been awesome at the hospital, and she was even better at home. She took good care of me, she prayed for me, and she made sure that I did my physical and speech therapy about ten times a day.

When she heard me moaning in pain, she was the first one to come to help me. Many times, she got up at two in the morning to make sure I was fine. She and I talked to each other using lip movements and facial expressions for three months, and she understood everything I said. Ann Angel transformed my inner and outer life completely. I felt that I had been born again, and I needed to fight back against my sickness and against any problem that came my way. It was not easy, but God had given me Ann Angel to support me. I could lean on her shoulder to control my pain and suffering. Without a doubt, Ann Angel had come from God to take care of me, to take me out of the hospital, and to bring me back home ill, but safe and sound. I used to ask Ann Angel and Margarita for drinks every hour because I felt I was burning inside for the heat was severe.

Going back to the first night I returned from Centinella Hospital, I asked Margarita for a glass of water. She hesitated to give me any drink because the nurses had put into her mind not to give me liquids to swallow, for I would choke. They gave her strict instructions to feed me liquids and solid foods only through the feeding tube. I never agreed, for I was positive I could manage to swallow. After I got home from the hospital, not once was I fed using the tube.

My friends left one by one around ten, and I began to see demons coming in to get me. I called Margarita and begged her to read the Bible for me. After she finished reading it, Ann Angel and Margarita prayed for a long time. They stayed up late making sure I would make it through the first night alive. They were afraid that I might not survive that night for I could not breathe, and I was very weak. I closed my eyes at around five in the morning, and I dozed off for about two to three minutes. Amazingly, that's all my body and spirit needed to give me strength, and to provide enough oxygen to my brain. I had asked Jesus in my prayers for a couple of minutes of sleep. He heard me and gave me what I asked him for, but it was enough to give me faith and hope for a speedy recovery. I had made up my mind that I wasn't going to go to any doctor or hospital to seek medical help. I'd rather die in my own bed with my two girls watching out for me.

I was convinced God had sent me Ann Angel to be my doctor, and that's all I needed. I also trusted more in Jesus that he was going to heal me at the right time. The feeding tube bugged me so much that I wanted to pull it out myself.

Before I got home, I knew I'd refuse to use it, and I made my choice: I was going to eat and drink by mouth the very first night I got back home from the hospital. I said to Margarita that I had to pay a last visit to a doctor only to remove the tube that I had attached to my flesh, which was already annoying me. Three weeks later, Ann Angel started helping me to write songs and this book that Danny Knus had begun.

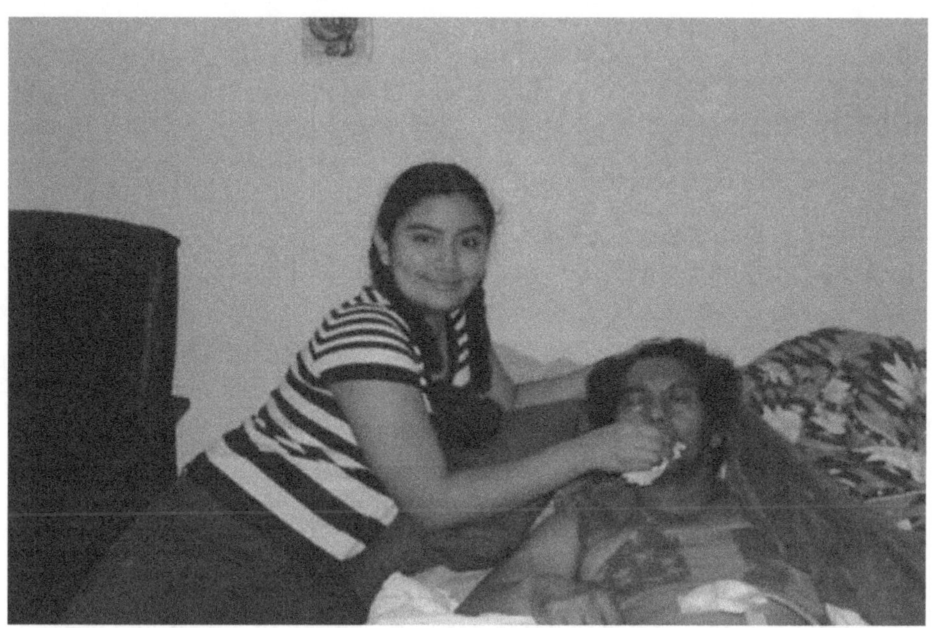

Ann Angel at home (February 11, 2017)

Margarita at home (February 11, 2017)

Best Friend

Several days had passed. I was trapped in my cage at home. I didn't get any better, my hope was dashing away, and doubts started to trick my mind. I wanted to talk, but no sound came out of my blistered mouth. I tried to roll my tongue and move my lips, but nothing happened. Margarita told me she was sure that I would never talk again. A couple of times, I heard her tell Ann Angel about her fears. Every time she talked about my illness with her friends and relatives, tears ran down her cheeks. And I cried along with her deep in my heart. I was sad to see that my family was suffering so severely.

On many occasions, I wrote notes in my notebook to encourage her that soon I was going to take care of them. I spent a lot of time praying with Ann Angel to motivate her and to bring her hopes, faith, and her self-esteem up. Margarita was working all the time and taking care of me twenty-four hours a day, seven days a week. But the money she brought home wasn't enough to pay the bills.

One night, I began to pray desperately, and I asked the Lord to take me with him or heal me soon, so I could work to help Margarita and Ann Angel. That night, I thought the end of my life had come. At one in the morning, Margarita hadn't returned from work yet. Ann Angel and Uriel, a good friend of mine, were babysitting me. I begged them to come to sit on the edge of my bed. A few days before, another good friend of mine had bought me a used hospital bed; I wasn't sleeping in my cage anymore. All of a sudden, my body got so hot that I felt I was going to be burn to ashes. Then, five minutes later, I got so cold, and I asked Ann Angel to cover me with five thick blankets. All the blankets piled up on me could not warm up my freezing body. I kept shivering and shaking, and my teeth were gnashing, grinding, and cutting my tongue and gums for my jaw was out of line. In my prayers,

I was asking for a few minutes of sleep to shut up my engine and stop thinking. When I was awake, my brain didn't send commands to stop the evil thoughts. Right away, God put me to rest, and I fell asleep for a few minutes. After the nap, Jesus showed me the kingdom of heaven. I saw the glory of God, the Creator of heaven and earth, the Lord who put my soul in a special place in my body, the Lord who hides my spirit somewhere where physicians and scientists are not able to see, to touch, or to study it. Chosen I am to see the house of God in a vision. And here's the vision: I saw myself flying over a special majestic garden in God's territory. I hovered over heavenly mountains and valleys. I was carried in the air by an invisible being to see the dwelling place of God, and his Holy Spirit was showing me the beauty of the formation of the Lord's mansion. Finally, it stopped above the top of the tallest most heavenly mountain resort to look down at the castle while I was still suspended, airborne. The Spirit of God revealed to my mind that I was watching the dwelling place of the master of the universe. I can't describe it in words, but the shape, the colors, and the design of the surroundings were awesome. In fact, I had been chosen to fly around the garden, and I saw the structure and design of the house of God, the Father and Creator of heaven and earth. In my spirit, I rejoiced for I felt the presence of angels guarding the whole divine premises of God's paradise. But I wasn't allowed to see any angelic being with my human eyes or with the eyes of my heart. Nevertheless, the Spirit of the Lord let me see the physical structure of the whole place. A few minutes passed, and my vision had ended, but my spirit had been filled with healing power. A couple of weeks were gone, and I didn't receive immediate healing. But I kept my trust in Jesus and I constantly prayed. One special night, I talked to the Lord for two hours. Suddenly, Jesus's presence was around me, I praised and thanked Him for visiting me. I stopped praying for a moment to listen to him. He remained quiet for a few seconds. Then, He gave strength to my flesh for several minutes. I was able to breathe properly for about three minutes for the first time since I got poisoned back on December 17, 2016, and I started to cry with happiness. All of a sudden, the voice of Jesus entered my mind, and I was told by the Lord, "Do not fear. Soon you're going to get well, you're going to be cured sooner than you think." Three weeks later, I moved my left thumb for the first time, and I spoke the first clear and understandable sentence for the glory of God. Two months after the vision, the impossible became a reality. Ann Angel and Margarita were already pushing me in a wheelchair. Every day, I got better and better; I started moving all my fingers, and with their help I stretched my legs. Soon I walked by myself with the support of a walker. In a short time, I tossed away the walker in spite of the doctor's objections. Healing started exactly as the Lord Jesus had told me several months before.

Satan Showed Up

Satan got very mad and jealous, and tormented me with fury. My quick healing provoked Lucifer to send an army of demons, and I received heavyweight punches from them. The devil feared, back in January, that Jesus would visit me soon. He also got worried that the Lord was coming to heal me. He started at the beginning of February to nail me to the cross. Mercilessly, he attacked me physically, spiritually, and legally. First, my body was covered with bruises and boils. Blisters, cuts, and rashes ate my flesh up. They couldn't even wash my face or my hands because my skin peeled off. I got severe irritations all over my back, stomach, and legs, and I had to spend a couple of weeks on my right side only, for they couldn't turn me over without bursting the blisters. I thought I had gotten modern-day leprosy. Then I got a terrible pain in all my joints. The joints on my left knee and on my right elbow swelled up. The pain was so bad that for many days I didn't move. My physical body was messed up.

Then my spirit came to an uncontrollable torment and affliction. I couldn't even pray because Satan was working on blocking my mind. Finally, I was falsely accused of a crime that I will talk about later in more detail.

The devil got into Henry to attack me. Henry brainwashed Margarita the first day he showed up at the hospital. He began to twist Ann Angel's mind during the audition for the "America's Got Talent" show held on February 11, 2017. In the first week of May, she would turn from Ann Angel to Wicked Anna, coming at full force to destroy me. In May, Ann Angel was going to become my worst enemy, and she would hate me so much that she would torture me, she would pin me to the wall. Her hate for me was going to be so strong and cruel that she wouldn't take care of me anymore. My sons, my brothers and sisters, my mother, my mother- in-law, and Margarita's sisters would join forces to destroy me too. They were not going to have pity on me, even though I was very ill, and I couldn't physically or mentally take care of myself. In May, Margarita and Ann Angel started to call me a liar. My sons and Henry told Margarita and Ann Angel the very first day they showed up at Centinella that I was faking the sickness. They told them that I had planned the whole thing, including the hacking. Henry and my two sons told them that I wasn't a truthful person. They implored Margarita to kick me out of her life because I was an evil husband and a bad and violent father. They told Ann Angel I had gotten the audition for her to participate in "America's Got Talent" to exploit her. I was planning on making her famous and then enslave her, as I had done it in the past with my sons. There and then, the venom was injected to Ann Angel and Margarita. Henry also told them that I had spoken with one of the top producers of the show, and he told me that he had a lot of faith in Ann Angel's singing talents. He put in their minds that I had signed an agreement with the producer to split all the money with him. He advised Ann Angel not to do well during the casting because I wanted to ruin her life if she made it to the finals. He briefed her on the day of the audition not to take care of me anymore. All of this happened on February 11, 2017, when Henry and Margarita took Ann Angel to the Los Angeles Convention Center where the auditions were held. I was at home, paralyzed and dying in my bed, but I was praying for her. Ann Angel's audition time was at 1:15 that afternoon, just four weeks after I was discharged from Centinella Hospital. During the audition, I saw a shadow person and dark beings following her around. I asked Jesus to take care of her, but the shadow man was around her all the time. I was able to see the shadow in my mind's eyes in my prayers. And my heart was beating me with emotional pain. I had the feeling that something wrong was going on at the audition. Henry and Margarita left for the audition at nine in the morning and more that twelve hours had passed. I was sad and worried, but I was still praying. My mother had stayed to take care of me. I had asked her to pray with me about five times. I was worried and waiting for news from them. Finally, they returned at 1:44 the next morning. Ann Angel came back tired and sad. She whispered several words, and in a couple of sentences she told me what had happened. I knew that everything had gone wrong from the tone of her voice. She was tired, and her words were broken, and she gave a defiant look at Henry. They all went to catch some sleep. My mother went back to her place after she said her last prayer. She blessed me and wished me a good night. Ann Angel asked me to bless her. I sent her to bed, and she gave me a kiss on my forehead.

Ann Angel got up at noon, and she came to check on me. She gave me my medication and sat on the edge of my bed crying. She talked to me for about an hour, to tell me what had happened at the "America's Got Talent" audition the night before. She warned me that Henry wanted to reduce me to dust. She said he had been nasty things to Margarita about me, and that she had overheard their conversation. Ann Angel also mentioned that her mom told her she had a plan to leave me in a few months, but she would never divorce me.

Ann Angel became even closer to me for the next ten weeks. She cried all the time, and we prayed together to ease her anguish. Since I couldn't speak yet, she led all our prayers. I promised her that I'd try my best to solve the problem, and that I was going to help her no matter what. I also assured her that when I'd get my voice back, if I ever spoke again, I'd talk to Margarita to tell her not to listen to my evil brother. She believed me, and we started to work together on the writing. I was still paralyzed, mute, and in bed, but I went back to the writing with the help of Ann Angel. First, I wrote a song that I called "Ann Angel." It took me about forty-five minutes one night when Jesus put the lyrics and the melody to my mind. The next day, I asked Ann Angel to get the guitar, and in less than an hour we had the chord progression ready to rock. She wrote the lyrics on the computer and recorded the melody on Pro Tools. Our song was completed in a couple hours, all because it was a gift from God. I have been asking him in every prayer to give me the gift of music because I had been tone-deaf. A month later, I had written and arranged ten songs. Two of them were Christian songs in English, two were Christian songs in Spanish, and the rest were Indie pop rock in English. I asked Jesus a special request to give me the lyrics to the best Christian song I could write. He granted my wish and he inspired me to write the lyrics for "Chosen I Am," which is my favorite Christian song. Satan kept a close watch to bury me alive, and he was ready to use relatives and family members to get to me.

One day, Lucifer entered into Ann Angel's heart. Suddenly Ann Angel went back to Anna my punisher. She refused to cook for me when I asked her to feed me, even though I begged her to have compassion for me. That was the beginning of my loneliness for the rest of my life. First, Henry stabbed me in the back for an unknown reason. Then Margarita joined and supported Henry to destroy me. In May, Ann Angel turned her back on me. On June 20, 2017, Ann Angel went on vacation to Nashville, Tennessee, and she never returned. I spent the next two weeks with Margarita, not talking to each other. She communicated with Henry all the time, and he told her what to do. I tried to convince her that he was going to destroy our family; even worse, he was going to ruin her life.

For ten weeks, I texted and called Henry, Tony, and Mario Jr. three to five times a day, but they didn't answer me. I couldn't understand why they hated me so much. Ann Angel, Jesus took back to heaven, but she would live in my heart forever. Anna left me for good, but she'll always be my precious earthly angel and my only daughter for the rest of my life. Certainly, they wanted to wipe me out. They came straight from hell to grind me and to burn my flesh and spirit alive. But I know Jesus shows me the way, teaches me the truth, and takes care of my life always and to the end of the world.

Summons Served

Hajiv Mhulay ended up in jail, but my close relatives continued to falsely accuse me. Even though I was improving physically—my paralyzed arm and my crippled leg were regaining movement after the stroke, and my voice was clearing up—Henry hired an army of evildoers to torture me. I had Jesus by my side, however. My Lord and Savior, Jesus Christ, kept rescuing me time and time again.

One night, Margarita and I went to church, and we were walking across the parking lot, when she received a text from Henry. I was surprised that she handed me over her cell phone to check the message after she read it. He suggested she go to court to file a spousal and child abuse claim against me.

After I read it, I became worried, and I grabbed her hand to keep my balance. She helped me to get back to the car. I sat and began to cry and pray. She stared at me with hate in her gestures and looks, but I invited her to pray with me. We drove away and went back home. It was around eight; she didn't say a word to me the whole night. She wept for a long time and fell asleep at about four the next morning, then at around seven she got up. She cooked and served me a special breakfast. I thanked her for the food and for everything else. I also begged her to forgive me for not being the best husband, and for all my errors and sins. I made her an invitation and asked her if she wanted to pray with me to thank the Lord for a new day. When we finished our prayer, she stood up.

She opened her mouth, and to my surprise, she said, "Can you forgive me, please for not believing you when you said that Henry is the enemy?" She rested her head on my shoulder, and she admitted that I hadn't done anything wrong to her, to my brothers, to my sons, or to anybody else. She gave me her word that she was going to take care of me, and we were going to be together for the rest of our lives. She promised me and herself that she would never talk to Henry ever again. He texted and called her many times every morning and every afternoon for two weeks, but she didn't answer him.

Henry was furious when Margarita stopped answering his calls and deleted his contact details for good. God showed me another miracle. I had lost my dear wife, and then she came back to love me, to care for me, and to glorify the Lord. Happiness showed on her face; I was glad that she got saved, and was on the Lord's side.

But Henry got very mad and called my sister-in-law and my mother-in-law to file a court order against me in the state of Tennessee. They manipulated Anna to testify falsely against me. On August 9, 2017, a phone call woke Margarita early in the morning. The call came from Nashville, Tennessee. A detective spoke with her and urged her to go to the police department in Los Angeles to put a warrant out for my arrest. He explained to her that Anna and her aunt had filed for child and spousal abuse against me in the court of Nashville, Tennessee. She refused to do it because she was a hundred percent sure of my innocence. The detective was very angry and subpoenaed her to show up in Nashville to testify in person. Margarita stayed with me four more weeks crying all the time. I encouraged her to go to Nashville and clear up all the mess because Henry, Maria, and Anna had gotten us into trouble. The last day came, September 7th, and that night at 8:15, I drove her to LAX and I waved her goodbye. We made a promised to each other that we would always be together no matter what, or how big the problems we had to face. We made it clear that we would talk every day to support one another. We had to live apart for an unknown period of time.

Days and weeks passed by, and we were true to our promise. But on the October 19, Margarita called me and told me that the social worker and the detective threatened to take Anna away if she didn't stop calling me. They forced her to cancel bank accounts we had together and to stop any physical, spiritual, and financial support she was giving me.

The detective had been tracking our conversations, getting information on our financial statements, and messing with our privacy and rights. I encouraged her to comply with the detective and the social worker's demands. Those were the final words I ever spoke to her; in life, we have to obey God's commandments first. Then we must follow and obey the law of the land to reach peace on earth and to have a small chance to enter the kingdom of heaven.

Tough Luck

The story of my life gets closer to its end, but my suffering won't stop. I've faced deadly diseases, and I've been hated all my life; friends, relatives, and family members have burned me alive many times. I've always been alone and ill. Now, I don't have a place to stay. I applied for social security benefits, but my application was denied twice. I tried to collect unemployment, but it wasn't approved either. A social worker and a detective in Nashville, Tennessee, forced Margarita and I to separate. Ann Angel was just an angel that Jesus sent temporarily to chase away demons that otherwise would have taken my soul to hell. Anna, my only daughter, doesn't want to talk or see me anymore, and the Tennessee Social Services Department banned me from seeing her and Margarita again. My two older sons don't respond to my emails or texts, so I stopped bothering them. I wish I could see and visit my seven-year-old son, Benjamin Matthew Revolori, but his mother and brothers don't allow me to get close to him.

March 15, 2014, five days after I married Margarita, Sonia Quinones my ex-wife, snuck into my house, she went straight to my room and forced the door to open it. She harassed Margarita and me and threatened me. In May 2017, she came one morning to my bed with a bunch of court ordered papers and asked me to sign them without reading them. She wanted to take advantage of my mental and physical illness. I tried my best to read them for my eyesight was improving. I refused to sign them because she wanted me to voluntarily give away Benjamin's parental rights forever. I have asked her many times to let me visit my son, Ben, but she doesn't answer me. I can only imagine, she says, "You're dead to me." I can't see or talk to my mother because she supports Henry, and she does whatever he asks her to do. I fear for my life. Henry and other close relatives are always looking for me; they wish me dead, and I fear they'll try to harm me again. All my brothers and sisters believe that I am the rotten apple of the family. Henry manipulates them, and they think I will spoil the bunch if I'm around them. I can't go back to work because I have a weak leg, severe vertigo, and my left arm is still paralyzed. But, in God I trust, because the Lord has told me, over and over again, in time, I'm going to heal completely.

Currently, Margarita lives in Nashville. She works at a hotel and she's doing great financially, but she's not happy without me. She is the best wife, the best mother, the best sister, and the best woman I have ever met. All I can say is that she's my best friend. She has the heart of an angel. She used to go out to help the needy with money, food, and clothes in the streets of Los Angeles. I'm honored to have shared my life with her. Truly, she was a gift from God, and she'll be my distant and imaginary friend for the rest of my life. Margarita once told me her tale.

Here's what she said: "In my early twenties, I had a dream; it wasn't just a dream, but a special revelation. I was told in my dream that I would marry two times. The first one would be for a few days. The second marriage would last for a lifetime. He would be the best man ever, but I was going to weep and suffer to stay by his side. Both husbands' first names would begin with the letter M. And it happened just as I dreamed. At the age of twenty-three, I met Michael. Then I married you, and we have lived four happy years together." Those were the words she told me on the way to LAX on September 7, 2017. And I hoped and prayed one day that this nightmare would come to an end, and she and I would be back together again.

But two months later, she changed her mind. On October 19, 2017, she called me and warned me that she wasn't going to talk to me anymore. According to her, the detective who was handling the spousal abuse case had told her not to communicate with me, but I didn't believe her excuse. She changed her phone number and all her social media accounts to stop me from contacting her. I became homeless on November 1, 2017.

On December 24, 2017, Fabiola, a lady who used to bring me food to the bus benches, texted my sons and asked them to pick me up because

I was dying on the streets, paralyzed, dizzy, and mute, eating stale food on the bus benches on First Street in East LA.

Mario Jr. replied, "We don't have time for him. We're busy celebrating brother Ben's birthday." I haven't talked to Anna, my sons, my mom, my brothers, or my wife ever since. They all banished me from their lives, and all the predictions Knus told me came true.

He was truly Nostradamus, the one who foretold the future of my life accurately.

All my relatives and friends abandoned me, except Fabiola. She took good care of me, buying me food and giving me a place to rest in her office. She's a friend Jesus chose and sent to support me, to ease my suffering and to take me wherever I need to go.

Hajiv Alair Mhulay Zhamgar in one of his threats wrote, "Your God is not powerful enough, and can't save you now." The Indian hacker, who tried to kill me, was arrested in Inglewood, California, on December 28, 2016, for he had mocked the God of Abraham, Isaac, and Jacob. He was handcuffed when he was trying to pass the main entrance at Centinella Hospital to go into my room. Margarita had told me that when emails came in the inbox and she watched the time, she felt demons were around her when the four digits were all ones. Three times she read them, when the clock showed 11:11 during the day, and at night on the clock at work, and on the stove timer at home. Those three times, she felt the presence of Satan trying to take and keep my soul. I kept wondering why she was so scared when she told me for the first time back in August 2016. Hajiv Mhulay was booked at exactly 11:11 in the morning on Wednesday, December 28, 2016. At 11:33, they locked him up. He was charged with the following violations: high prestige professional hacker, impersonator, computer breaker, sexual abuser, and attempted murderer.

Reports issued by FBI agent, Carlos Yuement, at 11:55 said the suspect requested to exercise his constitutional rights to make a call from jail. They granted his right, but instead of calling his lawyer or a close family member, he sent me his last email, which I read on September 5, 2017, when my vision had improved.

This is what he wrote: "Well, fine, you caught me. You also know what? I'm Indian, a hacker, and I'm not Stuart Stone. My name is Hajiv Alair Mhulay Shamgar, and you all have been played. I live in India and just wanted to f—— your hot daughter, you know! So what? That's what we do. We get into other people's f—— lives and destroy them. BTW, I impersonated Stuart Stone and I did meet Anna. I also got banned from coming to the US now, and it's all your fault! I was so busy tracking you that I got found and they banned me from coming."

The message went on with more threats and abuse against my wife and daughter.

The last report that the FBI wrote me was that Hajiv Mhulay had been extradited to his native India. Currently, he's serving a life sentence in Tihar Prison, near Delhi, India. Justice was finally served. I pray that one day, I can visit him in prison and show him love and tell him in person that I forgive him in the name of Jesus. I would also love to ask him why he attempted to kill me, and who paid him to poison me. I am sure I'll never find out his motive, unless Jesus shows me another of his awesome miracles. May the Lord have mercy and richly bless all my enemies. I pray for blessings and forgiveness for Henry, Maria, and for all those who got involved in hurting Margarita, Anna, and me. I don't know what I have done wrong for them to treat me that badly. I hope one day I learn the real reason why all my family members, relatives, and close friends hate me so much. As far as I know, I hold the record for surviving four different major strokes in forty years: the first at age nine, the second one in my early twenties, the third in my forties, and the last one provoked by poisoning in my fifties. To end the story of my life, I must say that I have been a fighter since I was a little boy running shirtless and barefoot in the fields of my village. I have recovered from many serious diseases, and I have solved all my problems because I've been a man of great faith. Praying all the time, forgiving, and eating healthy food have cured me of almost all my deadly diseases.

I was poisoned, I am still constantly tortured spiritually by Satan, physically by men, and falsely accused by my own close relatives, but I have always won, and I have a good winning attitude and go free because Jesus said, "I'm with you always, and I am the way, the truth, and the life." This is the truth, and no matter that I face dangerous toils and snares, and trials and tribulations that God allows the Devil, I'll follow Christ. Chosen I am, the Lord has sealed in my heart the gifts of forgiveness, love, anger management, fatherhood, and brotherhood. I will always tell the truth. And in God I trust.

M Gmail　　**Mario Quinones-Revolori <mario2qr@gmail.com>**

Why?

stuartstonecasting@yahoo.com　　　　　Wed, Dec 28, 2016 at
<stuartstonecasting@yahoo.com>　　　　　　　　11:55 AM
Reply-To: stuartstonecasting@yahoo.com
To: Mario Quinones-Revolori <mario2qr@gmail.com>

Well, fine, you caught me. You also know what? I'm Indian, a hacker and I'm not Stuart Stone. My name is Hajiv Alair Mhulay Zhamgar and you all have been played around. I live in India and just wanted to fuck your hot daughter you know! So what? That's what we do, we get into other people's fucking lives and destroy them. BTW, impersonated Stuart Stone and did meet Ana. I also got banned from coming to the US now, and it's all your fault! I was so busy tracking you, that I got found and they anned me from coming.

Thanks a lot motherfucker, you destroyed my entire life assholes!
You, your husband and daughter go to hell. You rhusband shall die in that hospital motherfuckers!!!

Hajiv Alair Mhulay Zhamgar

Visions and Revelations

It was a beautiful and clear morning on August 4, 2018, and the sun was shining brightly. I was still in bed praising and thanking God in my morning prayer. In a split of a second, I saw colorful heavenly beings around the universe, and I felt the presence of angels everywhere, but I didn't see them. I was contemplating the beauty of God's creation, when suddenly a dark cloud of gases rooted from the center of the earth, then moved up to enter heaven's door. The shape was so scary it looked like a rotten gigantic black mushroom. The Lord revealed to me that it was a nuclear bomb that the enemy had launched to destroy the whole planet.

Soon the dark gases covered the earth. In a short time, it began to fade and turn brownish. The hand of Jesus was everywhere, cleaning up the toxic fumes. Then I saw all kinds of sharp double-edged weapons filling up the sky, cutting everything and everybody to small pieces. They were flying, falling, and attacking from all directions. Again, Jesus battled the Antichrist, and the light began to shine for a little while. It was a fearful fight between good (Jesus) and evil (Satan) that the Lord allowed me to witness. At times, the whole universe was covered in darkness, the next minute the light was shining bright and clear. Jesus Christ established peace on earth for a little while. But God let me see the last fight Satan gave Jesus. He unleashed all the demons, monsters, and all his followers to fight and kill. It was the last time I saw the earth covered in darkness, and demonic beings destroying and killing people, animals, and burning every single plant. It was awful to see the earth and everything in it reduced to debris. In the end, Jesus defeated the Antichrist, and the Lord established his kingdom. There was peace forever, and the light never went out again. Jesus reigned on earth for eternity. Finally, Jesus created a new peaceful paradise, and a new Byzantine blue sky decorated with blue jewels, and diamonds hanging down from heaven over the new eternal City of Jerusalem. I kept listening and talking to the Lord. I thanked him, asked for forgiveness, and I blessed his holy name multiple times. I rejoiced so much that the Lord had listened to me singing my original song, "Chosen I Am" to glorify Him and to bless his holy name.

CHOSEN I AM

Son of God washed away the sins of the land
In his days he bled and took a stand
Good teacher gives me peace, love all-year
It's a chosen, chosen soul, and so I hear.

Chosen I am to pass heaven's gate
Sweet Lord let me in the seven doors
Write my name in the book, the book of life
It's a chosen, chosen soul, and so I hear.
Chosen I am.

Precious Lord, opened heaven's doorway wide
I arrived on the last soul's ride
Jesus shows me the way to pass; I'M is near
It's a chosen, chosen soul, and so I hear.

Chosen I am to pass heaven's gate
Sweet Lord let me in the seven doors
Write my name in the book, the book of life
It's a chosen, chosen soul, and so I hear.
Chosen I am.

Lamb of God wipes away my tears, I don't fear
I hear angels humming a heavenly song
Chosen I am and my soul sings along
It's a chosen, chosen soul, and so I hear.

///Chosen I am to pass heaven's gate
Sweet Lord, let me in the seven doors
Write my name in the book, the book of life
It's a chosen, chosen soul, and so I hear///
Chosen I am.

July 21, 2015

With Anna and her friend, Vallerie (August 2016)

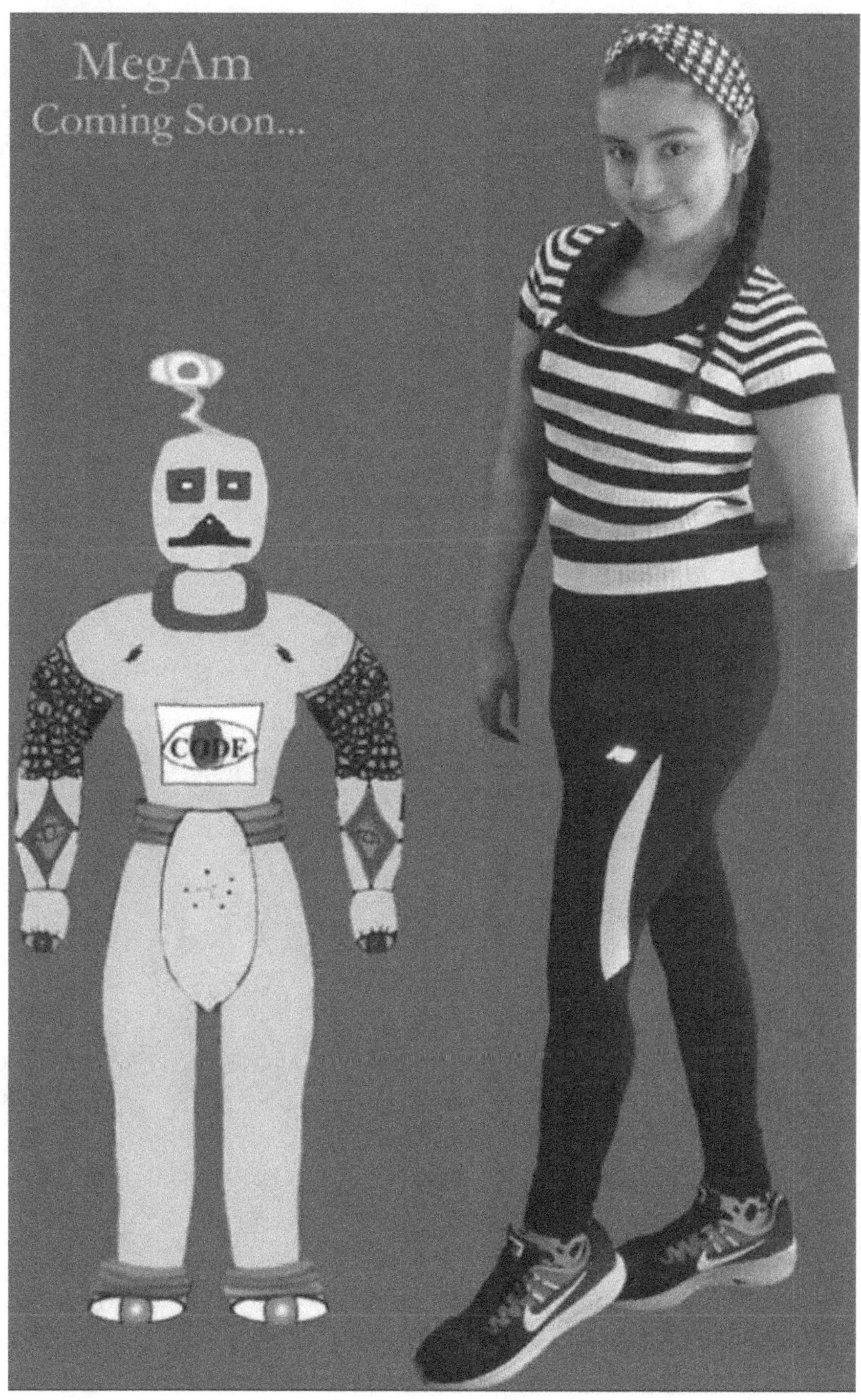

Superhero comic book character, MegAm (May 2016)

Off the wheelchair (May 2017)

With Henry, Margarita, and Nita (March 2017)

Birthday dinner (November 14, 2015)

Anna and I (2014)

Berlin, Germany

Berlin, Germany

Amsterdam, Netherlands

With Tony Revolori in Amsterdam (2014)

Copenhagen, Denmark (January 2014)

With Margarita, Mamma Rosa, and Papa Menche (December 2015)

*Anna at Pacifique Recording Studio with Grammy Award-winning
Ted Greenberg and Tony Valenciano.*

Anna and I (May 2014)

Anna and I shooting "The Cell" (May 2014)

With my son, Benjamin Revolori (November 2011)

Mario Revolori and Tony Revolori (November 2011)

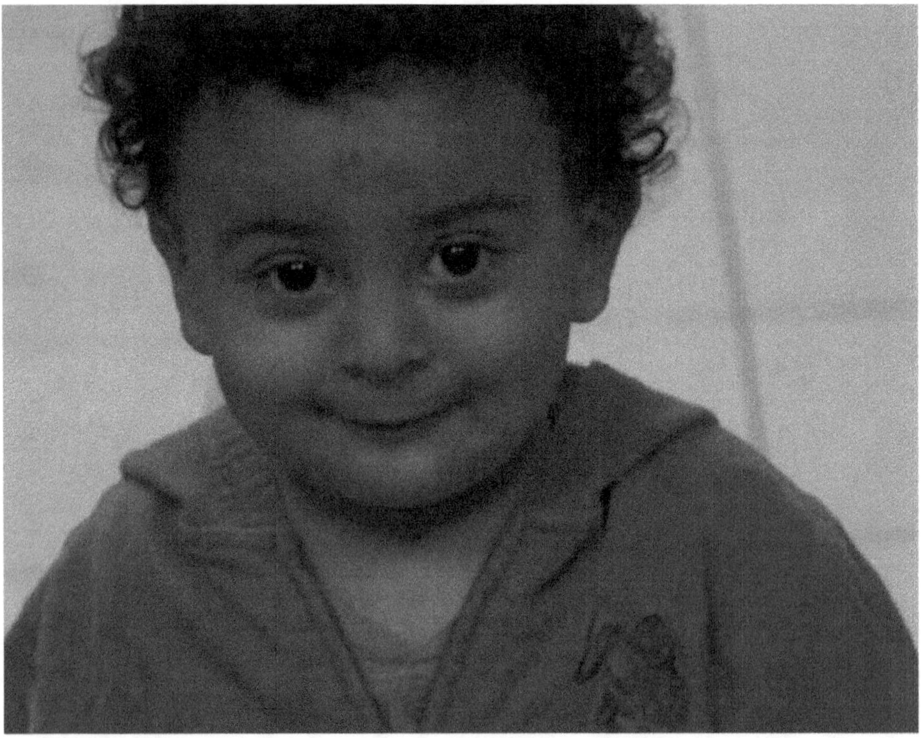

Benjamin Revolori (September 2011)

In my two sofas-bed cage (January 2017)